LETTERS TO JOHN GLENN

"P. S. I listened to your heartbeat"

LETTERS
TO
JOHN GLENN

With comments by *J.H. Glenn, Jr.*

Book Trade Distribution by
Doubleday & Company, Inc.

WORLD BOOK ENCYCLOPEDIA SCIENCE SERVICE, INC.
HOUSTON, TEXAS

ACKNOWLEDGMENTS

The publishers gratefully acknowledge the courtesy
of the following individuals for their permission
to reproduce facsimile portions of their letters,
and for the use of their names or signatures therein.

Mattie Ailstock
Mrs. Thelma F. Boullt
Gwendolyn Alyce DeYoung
Anatoly F. Dobrynin
Faye Farley
Bob Hope
Wendy Kaufman
Frances Marg
Kathleen McVey and friends

Joan Monas
Bayla Ness
Stanley E. Rosen
Albert Rosenberg
Philip Rosenzweig
Alan Sinsheimer
Robert W. Whitee
Frank Wurth, Jr.

CONTENTS

ILLUSTRATIONS

"TO STEVE"

Lively, gregarious, friendly, emotional, and helpful are all words that would describe Steve Grillo. When the occasion arose, efficient, brusque, and thoughtful might also be appropriate. Steve was a "take-charge-guy" whose task it became to establish order out of the chaotic influx of mail, and in his position as Director of Administrative Services for NASA Headquarters, he did just that.

His interest, however, was not just one of establishing cold, clerical efficiency, for Steve's interest in people was not only in terms of so many thousand per mailsack, but as individuals who placed their innermost thoughts and feelings on paper and sent them to me. He shared with us more of the elation, emotion, and personal human feelings that were expressed in the mail than any other person.

As the self-appointed Postmaster of the "Glenn Post Office," Steve was equally at home in such diverse tasks as making certain that an injured boy had an immediate answering letter, that an English scientist had his letter forwarded by us to his proper American counterpart, that threatening crank mail was sent to the Postal Inspector, or that a wonderful woman on Long Island was invited to Washington for part of the farewell ceremony and was treated to the Steve Grillo "royal tour" because she sent me a hand knitted five by seven foot American flag.

Steve was what I would term an active patriot, proud of his Army record and his participation in the Reserve Officers Association, proud of his participation in civic organizations, and proud of his lengthy government service.

Steve died in May of 1963. Along with many other people, we lost a good friend. His example of empathy, warmth, and understanding set an example we could well follow.

To Steve Grillo, "Postmaster Without Portfolio," this book is dedicated.

FOREWORD

☆ ☆ ☆ ☆ ☆ ☆ ☆ ☆ ☆ ☆ ☆ ☆ ☆

Three gray United States mailbags sat in the middle of the living room floor and beside them was a crate of fresh eggs. This was my first return home following the earth-orbital space flight of Friendship 7 in February of 1962, and to say that I was surprised to see these additions to our Early American style living room is an understatement.

The preceding days, remember, had been wonderful and full days for me and my family. The orbital flight took place on February 20th and after two days of debriefing at Grand Turk Island, I had returned to Cape Canaveral for more debriefing, a press conference and ceremonies with President Kennedy and Vice-President Johnson.

The family and I had spent a restful weekend at Key West, Florida, and had then flown to Washington with the President on Air Force One for a reception at the White House, a parade down Pennsylvania Avenue on a rainy day, and a joint meeting of Congress. Following the Congressional meeting we had a luncheon at the State Department. Only later did we return to our home in Arlington, across the river. Needless to say, it was good to be home.

Our initial reaction to the mailbags was to open them—which we did. I thought this was probably all the mail we had received, but when a postman came to the door and told me the Post Office was holding approximately a truck-load of additional mailbags, I realized the three bags that friends had placed in our living room were just a token of what actually had arrived.

It was a hectic scene, as you can imagine. People coming in and going out the front door. Neighbors dropping in to welcome us home. Telegrams arriving. Radio and TV people still covering our homecoming. In general, the place looked like a pandemonium scene in a movie.

But we did want to see what was in the mail, so we all sat on the floor for a little while and opened letters in the first installment of what was to become a real avalanche.

Even at that early time, we were impressed by the variety of mail. There were telegrams and cables, there were proclamations coming in from towns, cities, and communities. There were citations and notices of an official nature from governments. There were gifts and other small packages. Letters that began "From Her Royal Highness" of such and such, or "From His Majesty" of somewhere. There were messages from all kinds of government agencies, from officials all over the world, and from all levels of governments.

But outweighing such official documents were the thousands of letters from people who had lived through the whole experience with me and my family. And these were the messages that really gave us the heart-warming feeling of closeness to so many people, the feeling we were to know over and over again.

It soon became obvious we could not begin to open and sort all of the mail personally. Fortunately, Mr. Steve Grillo, one of our friends in the Administrative Services Division of NASA Headquarters, foresaw what a problem this was to become and took steps to organize and handle the mail. Thanks to his efforts and those of his assistant, Mrs. Amelia

Leukhart, we were able to cope with this responsibility.

Steve died in early 1963. I am sorry he could not add some of his own observations to these pages, for he was a friendly, most human individual who loved people and thoroughly enjoyed our sharing with him the sentiments sent to us in the mail.

The orbital flight of Friendship 7 was so well covered by the press and television that many people literally did "live through" the whole event with us. And when they shared our delays, disappointments, and successes, they felt they just had to let their feelings be known—and we appreciated hearing from these many friends.

One young gentleman phrased it rather well when he said, "In our class we listened on the raido to your flight. It was very seccesfully. We were very happy. I felt like it was a mew world." After a few other statements, he finished with a short poem that I'm sure describes the feelings of many people: "Roses are red/vetols are blue/when you went around the wrold/we did to." And then following the poem, he added, "We are thankful for all the sinestists who made the flight secesfully." I think that many people felt that same way. They actually had gone around the world with me that day in Friendship 7.

Another young lady in grade 5 opened her letter with the following grammatical massacre, "The day you were shot, I watched you go up on TV in school." But she continued with a wonderful letter of what the flight meant to the class and to her personally.

This book is not to be a recounting of the specific events during or following the flight. It is rather to let you, after a fashion, look over our shoulders as we opened the mail. Most of the mail we opened was congratulatory in nature and we appreciated it very much, but this is not a collection of congratulations. As time went on, we began to notice a small percentage of letters that were out of the ordinary. These ran the gamut of human emotion and experience which we found very interesting, and I think you will, too.

To clarify, the letters we have selected for this book are *not* the usual run of letters. They are from a small percentage of the mail that we termed "special interest." This is not meant to be just a "funny book" of letters as the Table of Contents indicates. There are many, many categories that the mail covered. But these are a few of the unusual—the unusual that we found especially interesting. We have tried to excerpt the interesting parts of letters, for to publish all of every letter would make this book too voluminous.

In February, 1964, I was injured in a fall and was forced to spend several months in a convalescent status. During that period we decided that if these letters were of special interest to us, we could put a few of them into a book and share them with others. We sifted through only a small number of the two hundred and fifty to three hundred thousand letters received to date. It's obvious that to do otherwise would require a large editing staff. So these letters are samples taken from a few thousand letters along with a few to President Kennedy that he had forwarded to us from the White House. There would be many more just like them, or probably better examples, if we had gone through all the mail. While most of the mail was congratulatory and concerned directly with space flight, other letters covered such fields as politics and our relation to the President, the international effect of the flight, religion in the form of praise for what we have said about our own beliefs or feelings, and crank letters from religious people who felt that we should not be doing what we were doing—exploring space. Many people have sent in religious tracts, faith healing advice, and all manner of things connected with religion. A portion of the mail has been concerned with our interest in the Boy Scouts and the YMCA, youth work, and church groups.

Some of the mail was interesting because of unusual addresses by which the mail arrived. These included such variations as just a picture on an envelope dropped into the mail, or another one listed as Glenn, USA. Some people have written sharing their troubles with us or have wanted to give medical advice to me since I was injured. Many people are interested in ancestry or finding out if we are related. There have been many namesakes. These have included not only individual names of infants, but names of schools, institutions, and a variety of organizations. Other people have submitted inventions, manuscripts, or songs that they wanted help in getting published, or offered investment proposals showing how they thought we could all become rich by one means or another.

Some people have assumed, because we had a measure of success in the space program, that we were now an overall authority on many different areas, including economics, banking, investment, and almost as many things as you can think of. Others have severely criticized me for things they did not like. To become the focal point for some persons' feelings on such things as racial problems or political dissatisfaction is sometimes startling. Thousands of requests have been received for pictures and autographs—autographs on stamps, on first-day covers and on every kind of material on which I could write.

Each of the letters was answered—not very promptly in some cases I'm afraid, and I hope there weren't many we missed.

Let me point out that I certainly do not want to embarrass anyone who wrote to us, nor to betray their confidences. For that reason, names have been omitted (except for certain letters) and certain place names have been changed.

But that is the only thing that has been changed; the wording, and in some cases the misspellings and errors are exactly as received in the mail.

This is not meant to be just a "funny" book. Some letters are funny, but others reflect the special interest mail that is sometimes pathetic, or humorous, or from people who obviously have a mental imbalance, or are sick physically. Most of the mail, though, came from just wonderful Americans who wanted to be associated with what had occurred, and to express themselves personally to us.

One phrase reflects the general nature of the mail received and of the way many people consider our relationship. They feel they lived through so many big events and big days with us that they felt much as the little girl who finished her letter with "P.S. I listened to your heart beat." They did, both figuratively and literally. In turn, I listened to the "heartbeats" of many people through their revealing letters.

But enough of this introduction. This book is not a sociological study. It has no particular message or theme, and perhaps a more definitive study can be made at a later time. This is rather an attempt to let you see some of the things we found out of the ordinary and of special interest in our mail. So picture yourself sitting on our living room floor with a good letter opener and . . .

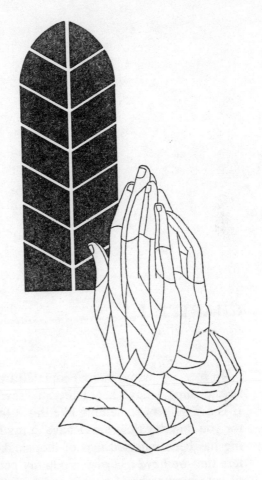

"THE HAND OF GOD..."

CHAPTER 1

In meeting many, many people all over the country there is one thing I have heard literally several thousand times. It is a statement something like this, "John, I prayed harder for you that day than I ever have in my life." This same feeling has been reflected tens of thousands of times in the letters that we have received. To many people, this was a time of returning to basic beliefs and feelings, and they wanted to let us know what it had meant to them.

Another notable thing about the religious mail has been its non-denominational character. While I am Protestant and Presbyterian, there has been an almost proportional distribution of letters from Catholics, Jews, Mormons and even some from other religious faiths such as Islam and Buddhism.

There was a feeling of "oneness," a desire to share with, and help, a fellow human being that transcended mere religious form and denominational lines. Though these prayers came from many people, in many lands, in many religions, in many sects, in many languages, and in many forms, I can't help thinking they sprang from the same source of inspiration, power, and guidance.

How do you tell someone you appreciate their prayers to God on your behalf? I guess the only really effective thing we can do is to join with them and continue to add our prayers to theirs.

From a Woman in Johnstown, Pennsylvania

I'm very happy that you made such a successful journey into space, John, but if you had continued on up to heaven, I know you would have been equally as welcome.

From a Nun in Buffalo, New York

This atomic generation can use your vocabulary. We hope and pray they absorb as readily the manly traits you display. You represent the "American Image" we wish them to portray in their adult lives. A man's real achievement is the conquest of self. On that score we agree that Colonel Glenn is truly "Go".

3

When Heaven replaces earth as your home we are sure that Christ, too, will extend His Hands in welcome. Our imagination can picture Him saying to you, Colonel, "Welcome Aboard, Sir!"

From a Group of Evangelists

"GOD WROUGHT SPECIAL MIRACLES BY THE HANDS OF PAUL, SO FROM HIS BODY WERE TAKEN HANDKERCHIEFS AND APRONS, AND DISEASES DEPARTED FROM THEM, AND EVIL SPIRITS WENT OUT OF THEM":

Read Acts 19th chapter, 11–12 verses.

Place this ribbon on your body and keep it there. We have prayed over it and we believe God will anser prayer. You will see the hand of God as it meets your needs, Spiritually, Physically, and Financeually.

Write your testimony and send it to us and we will put it in our Monthly Bulletin.

"THE PRAYING HANDS PRAYER BAND"

From a Social Security Number
—No Name—in Cleveland, Ohio

From the very beginning of the Mercury Program, I have had a strong sense of identification with you. We are both Ohio natives, I suspect our ancestry is similar, we are about the same age—oh, there are a dozen or more reasons why I felt that you, in your tiny

4

enclosure, represented me more than did any of the other astronauts. And when the count-down reached the 10-second mark, I dropped to my knees and began to pray. I am not much of a church-goer, but somehow I felt this was a thing between you and me and God. It was the least I could do, and at the same time it was the most I could do. And I like to think that perhaps my prayer was the last hundred-thousandth of one percent that made the difference between the spectacular success that was, and the failure that would have been too horrible to contemplate.

From a Woman in Harrisburg, Pennsylvania—to Mr. and Mrs. John Glenn, Sr.

I would like to share with you my testimony of believing, accepting and receiving the Lord Jesus as my own personal saviour.

I left home in my late teens for over a year. I lived in sin, lying, cheating, smoking and drinking. I ended up by having a child out of wedlock. Having this child made me stop and do a lot of thinking. Where did life really begin? Where does it end? What lay beyond death's door? Would a loving God let me into heaven with what I have done?

I started reading my Bible from beginning to end, but try as I might I just couldn't understand it and yet my sinful life was a torment to me. I decided to have a talk with my minister. We had a short talk. He said he thought God would overlook my first mistake and I wasn't the first person on earth who did this and I wouldn't be the last. So thinking he knew God and God's way, I tried to forget my past. I went on to get married, my husband adopted my baby. I had two more children, but deep down in my heart the fear of dying and meeting God stayed. Where was I really going to spend eternity?

One day I met a neighbor who testified of her salvation. I started once again reading my Bible only this time I didn't want a church or a religion or anything false. I wanted a lot of answers to my many questions and I could only get these answers by reading my Bible and praying to God and asking Him to give me understanding in what I was reading.

5

And when I opened my heart and asked God to have mercy on my soul and to forgive me of my sins in Jesus' name, God answered. "Though your sins be as scarlet they shall be as white as snow" Isaiah 1:18

On August 5, 1960 I was born into the family of God (John 3:3) "Verily, verily I say unto thee except a man be born again he cannot see the kingdom of God." Friend we must all have this born again experience. There is only one way and that's God's way.

I have had trials and tribulations since then, but I also have what I longed for, peace in my soul and joy unspeakable, more so, when I share with others my testimony.

Telegram from a Woman in Dallas, Texas

Food for thought. What effect will your hospitality to atheist Titov have on young Americans?

From a Mother in Colonia, New Jersey

I thought you would be interested to know that while we watched the rocket blast off this morning on the television my six year old son said: "Mom, I think we all should say a prayer." He then led his younger sister and me in the audible repetition of The Lord's Prayer.

At the request of Paul, I'm enclosing the picture of the capsule atop the rocket and the earth he drew today in his kindergarten class.

To you and Mrs. Glenn, and to your two fine children, we extend our very best wishes. God bless you all.

Parents from Michigan Write:

We wanted to pass onto you a prayer our 6-year-old John, Jr. sent along your way among many others. Some of the names are a little mixed up however, the meaning was there.

"Oh God we thank you for John Glenn who went around our whole United States World three times. We are so very thankful his capsule didn't get on fire but that you brought him back safe to Cape *Canaveral*. We also thank you for bringing back safe Roger Shephard and, and the other guy. Oh God we are thankful that the men the Russiantons sent up came back safe too! AMEN."

From a Woman in Freehold, New Jersey

I want to thank you for the wonderful thing that you have done for our country.

For some reason I had not really thought too deeply of what your flight means to us, as free people. Then this morning, at Mass—it seemed to hit me all at once. The priest gave a wonderful sermon based on your flight. In effect he said, that but for the Grace and Will of God—a miracle such as took place this past week would never have been possible.

This makes me realize just how little we know—you, me, President Kennedy, anyone compared to the great knowledge that our Father has. It has made me realize first how completely our lives are in the hands of Him.

I believe that God will allow us to go on exploring space—and giving us men such as you and your fellow astronauts to help us. I pray that someday we will have world peace. Yet if all this should end in war and destruction of the world then I will know, and accept that it was not meant to be.

7

From a Man in Baltimore, Maryland

Major Glenn, I was prompted to write you after reading an article in Reader's Digest titled "Moscow Radio Broadcast, Christmas, 1960."

I quote, "Our rocket has by-passed the moon. It is nearing the sun, and we have not discovered God. We have turned the lights out in heaven that no man will be able to put on again. We are breaking the yoke of the Gospel, the opium of the masses. Let us go forth, and Christ shall be relegated to mythology."

Certainly, I, being a Christian cannot believe that. So I write you, Astronaut John H. Glenn, Jr., in the hopes that you will after your earth-orbital trip write to me and in your own words tell me what your answer is to the above Russian statements.

Telegram from a Man in Brooklyn, New York

Greetings Your Honesty and truth is God's Blessing beware of Khruschev and Titov a liar and cheat of the world.

From a Nonbeliever in Moroni, Utah

I am one of the more than 180,000,000 Americans who thrilled at your wonderful accomplishment in orbiting the earth. I have great regard for the courage, the devotion, and the fine efficiency which you brought to this very specialized task.

But when you delve into the world of the metaphysical, your distinctions disappear and you are just another bewildered and anxious mortal like the rest of us, and guilty of the same banalities, speculations, and misconceptions which bedevil all of us in this illusive and elusive field.

I refer, of course, to your article in the current Reader's Digest, "WHY I KNOW THERE IS A GOD." Col. Glenn, you DON'T know there is a God! Ordinarilly, it would be a very rash and reckless statement for one man to tell another what the other does or does not know. But in this instance you furnish the evidence upon which you base your "knowledge" of God, and since that evidence is distorted, misinterpreted, mere heresay, and worthless, it is safe to assume that the conclusion drawn from it is equally faulty.

But let's give you the benefit of every doubt, and assume, as you do, that because of the magnitude, complexity, diversity, etc., of the universe "it couldn't just have happened". Let us also follow your concluding step and assume that instead the universe was created by a God (omniscient, omnipotent, and omnipresent, of course, because I do not presume you are inventing a God of your own). Does this then solve our original problem? Certainly not! It merely compounds and farther confuses it. For if reason demands that the simpler existence (the universe) "could not just happen" then it is anarchy of reason to assume that the far greater magnitude, complexity, and diversity, (God) "could just happen." And if, in conformity with our own established reasoning, God could not just happen, are we not involved in a far more complex and less soluble problem?

Again, you say, "It is the ORDERLINESS of the whole universe about us" by which you KNOW there is a God. The universe is NOT orderly! It is disorder; it is confusion; it is chaos!

For instance, two billion years ago, more or less, our own world came into being because of a cataclysmic DISORDER—and a great explosion of matter which sent it swirling, a ball of fiery gases into unchartered space. Thousands of just such cataclysmic DISORDERS occur each year, many of them dwarfing our own planetary system. Some of them have seriously affected our own planet, and that it has so far escaped annihilation is merely due to the vagaries of chance.

And of course this "order" you find in the universe does not include the important sidereal revolution of our earth because it is so awkward and so disorderly that the inventive genius of our age has not been able to come up with a calendar which will coincide with it.

But coming down to matters which do come within the compass of our "foot of twine" we note the "disorders" of earthquakes, tidal waves, typhoons, hurricanes, droughts, floods, frosts, lightenings, and plagues, which destroy life indiscriminately, the good and bad, the rich and poor, the old and young, the deserving and underserving, babes and women, and the helpless creatures, all in a senseless and purposeless havoc that is an affront to reason, to justice, and to all the virtues within human conception.

9

And is not the earth itself a glaring example of senseless and purposeless creation? Even its limited land expanse is less that one fifth arable; by no stretch of the imagination could one third of it be considered a suitable habitation for man. It is compounded largely of excesses—heat, cold, moisture aridity. It is bedeviled by every type of germ, parasite, weed, vermin, and they seemingly have a survival factor many times superior to our own. Man's survival and advancement is measured directly by the degree to which he can circumvent, thwart, counteract, or modify the "orderliness" of the universe—or adapt himself to the vagaries of its operations. It NEVER adapts itself to the needs nor the desires of its human creatures!

Lastly, there is life itself, and here the *disorders,* the senseless waste, the brutality of its endurance, it is so hideous that one our current commentators, commenting on the endless torture and suffering of lower life forms, and the gruesome destruction of it in senseless excesses, says, "We say that to the reasoning being Nature offers all the proofs we need that no consicous superior Power exists, but if there were such a power, it would be the most fiendish monster we could think of."

And is it not remarkable that our atheist friends, the Russians, who orbited farther, faster, and first, and just as safely, found no evidence whatever of the existence of a God?

No, Colonel Glenn, God is the man-made answer to the question of ultimate origin, and it answers not at all since the answer to ultimate origin is beyond the conception of the human mind. About any God, his plans and his purposes, you and I KNOW exactly the same, which is absolutely nothing!!! I admit this; you prove it!

From a Woman Volunteer in a V.A. Hospital

No, you most certainly were not alone as you zoomed around the world.

I'm a volunteer escort at the V. A. Hospital and I hadn't realized how many were with you, with their minds and their hearts, until I walked down empty hospital corridors and found my patients in the T.V. room, or, when I'd go after another in P.T. (Physical Therapy), and 1st thing, no matter how bad he was feeling he'd ask where John Glenn was?

One patient on a litter who had holes bored in his head and another hole in his neck, he could not raise or set up, asked me to leave him at the T. V. room. I asked him if he was sure he could see the T.V. and he said "yes," if I'd have the nurse hand the mirror over his stretcher.

Other patients with no arms or no legs, which they had given for their country, were in the T. V. room and the blind were listening, and all the patients in their hearts were with you every inch of the way.

I could feel the silent prayers, as I looked over the groups of men, some having nothing much left to their bodies but their hearts, yet, they were thinking of you and not of their miseries.

No, you were not alone.

From a Woman in Portland, Oregon

While you were circling the globe, the thought entered my mind that if Satan was cast "down to Earth", then you fellas out in orbit, beyond the Earth's gravity would be out of Satan's jurisdiction, and should there be life on other planets they would not be living in sin.

It's something to think about anyway.

A pleasant thought at that, huh?

From a "Tough Boss" in New York City

It's not hard for me to write, but it is difficult for me to explain who I am and why I write.

Who am I?

11

I am head of a relatively small company and probably regarded by all but a few as a hard bitter, tough boss with no emotions.

I am an Air Force Veteran who has twice been in a plane in flames and who has three times landed in an airplane without benefit of wheels.

I am a married man of sixteen years standing, with five kids (13 and under) who loves my wife and my five kids.

I am an Irishman by descent (on both sides) with some of the toughness and some of the sentimentality that goes with this heritage.

I am a publisher (by trade) with all the objectivity (or cynicism, if you like) that goes with making your way in this unusual communications business. I have technically seen everything in the way of a story—that is, until today!

I am a Catholic and I love my religion, not because I am a religious man, or a good man, but because I need God's help, and, because God is so good He offers it, so I constantly ask for it.

Today, when I heard you were probably going to go, I went off to early Mass, took Communion, and prayed for the success of your mission. I live 50 miles from the City and commute daily (not tonight because I had a very important commercial engagement). When I realized you wouldn't blast off until 9:45, I put a small radio in my pocket, got on the Railroad, and whipped into the City.

I prayed the most powerful prayer I know (the *Memorare*) in the last minute before you "blasted off" and for the first time in a day, when, often, I was to find tears in my eyes, I wept at the very magnitude of the job you faced. I think my tears were really for the extraordinary demonstration of Faith in God and in yourself that this mission so effectively demonstrated.

In any case, the magnitude of what you were doing and what you ended up doing so successfully, was so beyond my comprehension that I was alternately in tears and smiles all day long.

I'm sure I'm not alone—but I may be one of the few, among the many, who try, so inadequately, to express to you my deep thanks to God, that He was with you all the way, and my thanks to you for what you have done today for all of us in America, not so much in a scientific way, as in a spiritual way.

The scientific demonstration was the most superb I have ever witnessed. It was sensational, dramatic, dynamic and gave us hope that it wouldn't be too long before we were back on top of the scientific progress heap.

But far more important to me, and I am sure to millions others of us, Americans, was the spiritual demonstration of your faith in yourself, in your project, and in God.

For this demonstration, for the tears of realization I had to wipe away all day, I thank you. Your entire time in space and your safe return was one great prayer based on a great faith and I thank you for that, too.

From a Macy's Saleswoman

I am only a shoe saleswoman in Macy's Dept. Store in N.Y.C. But I want to thank you for your splendid courage in doing for the U. S. What you accomplished I want you to know that all of Macy's was in thoughts and prayed for you all through your trips.

From a Mother of Three

It seems an imposition to write to you as we know how busy and exciting these days must be for you all but still we feel such an affinity to you that even though this letter is never read I feel compelled to put into words what it all meant to me, to mine and to those around us.

Do you have any idea, Colonel, how close we were to you in those last moments of countdown? It was a soul-shattering experience beyond human description. Five minutes before lift-off I asked my six-year old Mark if he would pray with me for you and the mission. "Mama," he said quietly, "I already have." Through those last heart-stopping seconds there was an almost holy feeling in the room as we each in our own way beseeched our Lord to take care of you. I've wondered since then, if all the prayers of the people could be printed on a tape and stretched into miles if they, too, might not girdle the earth. Our thoughts were for you, too, Annie; for if we felt this way, how must you be feeling?

This letter is to thank you, John, for offering up your life so willingly for your country. I've always loved and been proud of my country. Surely there are bad things and evil deeds here but they lie in the giant shadow of good, fine and brave deeds that hover over our land. I will always say the same, good or bad, success or failure.

13

Pray that all the adulation a sometimes foolish public can bestow will not change you or your family situation one bit. The first time you get kissed by a devastating movie star I hope it's not on TV because I'll be sick to my stomach! Sometimes I think TV is an x-ray of the human soul as it shows so much more than it is supposed to. Those first seconds of liftoff, the moments before you were in orbit, the endless hours of circling, the heart stopping tension of re-entry and the, thanksgiving and relief. Oh, yes, Glenn, you wrote on our hearts in indelible ink that will not fade in a life time. I feel, too, that during those most dangerous moments of the journey when all the overwhelming efforts of science, the endless training and preparation down to the most minute detail hung in the balance and line between success and disaster was drawn exceeding fine that God, too, was at the helm in answer to all of our prayers and brought you safely home to Annie and your family, a kind of "spiritual booster" as it were.

We stand on the threshold and the door of space slowly, begrudgingly swings opens. And there's John Glenn, of New Concord, Ohio, U.S.A., Earth, giving it a good healthy shove.

From a Man in Pasadena, California

I believe if the nations of the world will go along with God, and show a sign that they are trying for world peace, God will go along with the nations. "Remember how the Indians use to sit in a circle, and smoke their peace pipes?" They were spreading confidence among each other, were in harmony with each other. This was a symbol of peace which got more effect than if they had just run back, and forth, to each other talking peace. That is what the nations are doing today, just talking peace back, and forth, to each other. "When you told your wife you loved her, it didn't give her the security that the engagement ring did." When you put the ring on her finger that cinched it. That is what is needed among the nations. Something more than just talks, and promise. I am thinking of a ring, a symbol of peace. Something concrete giving evidence of their sincerity, not just words, treaties, and promises. "All nations throw their hat into the ring. Just a little effort for the world's greatest cause, World Peace." Every nation, each nation, take some of their ships, and place them in the oceans so far apart. Each nation joining their ships in a complete circle around the earth, making a circle, a ring of world peace.

P.S. If you like this idea I wish you would talk it over with President John F. Kennedy.

From a Woman in Florida

I know you are still wondering about those tiny objects that you mentioned on TV and what they could be. Most of us know and we want you to know that they were our Hail Mary's floating around you to let you know our blessed Mother and her Son were watching over you.

From a Sixth-Grade Girl in Greenville, South Carolina

On reading the fourth Book of Kings we learn that Elias took off in a fiery chariot many thousands of years ago; and, as far as anyone knows he is yet extended in space, awaiting the last day
Maybe on your next trip, you can give an eye to Elias and ask him to share some of his Space secrets.
Could the fire flies be sparks from his chariot?

15

To President John F. Kennedy—
From a Man in Mt. Pleasant, Michigan

I enclose a copy of a prayer which my sister of Mt. Vernon, Illinois, showed to me on a recent visit with her. I thought it would be of interest to you and Col. John H. Glenn, Jr. because of the circumstances surrounding it.

My sister has a daughter who is twelve years of age. She belongs to a little club consisting of eleven other girls and herself—all of whom are about the same age. The evening before Col. Glenn's historic space flight this group met at my sister's house, and when everything seemed unusually quiet in the room where they were congregating my sister looked into it and found all of them on their knees with hands folded and reciting this prayer which they later told her had been made up by them that evening.

I thought it a fine commentary on the youth of America believing it is typical of the majority of them. I would like to suggest a television address by you directed specifically to them and covering what you consider to be the important aspects of the future of our country and setting forth the role which they can play in it. I believe such an address would be most helpful and effective if good advance publicity were given to it.

Pray for America

Please dear God, listen to
America now as he reaches toward the enlightenment,
keep him safe; keep him safe there,
enlightening and bring
him back alive. Deliver us
and keep us safe &
prove there is ever more
compassion in our
prayers.

Amen.

From a Sunday School Class in Riverside, Ontario

We are talking about you in our Sunday School.

Your church has the first name as our church.

We are all going to say the same prayer for you just as your rocket ship blasts off.

It is the closing prayer we say at Sunday School.

> *"Thank you God for this new day*
> *Thank you for our work and play*
> *Thank you for the sunshine too*
> *Thank you God for all you do."*

Don't be afraid when you are up there because we have asked God to help you . . . If you see God please say we love him . . . Take some candy with you in case you get hungry . . . Don't forget to say your prayers at night . . . Your little boy sure is lucky . . . Drive carefully . . . Don't forget your handkie.

From a Woman in New South Wales

I feel I must write and let you know of my experience on the night of February 24th, 1962. Whilst watching television with my sister and my husband.

It was your flight into space we were watching. Sometime later your photograph was flashed upon the screen and while the announcer continued talking about your flight, etc., etc., I suddenly became aware that there was another face on the screen, immediately behind your right shoulder. I watched the face for some moments before realizing it was the face of Christ and he appeared as a living person. I then asked my sister if she could see anything strange on the screen. She said, "Yes, I can."

I, then, asked her to describe to me fully what she could see. She, then, said "it's a man's face", then described every little detail about it. It was exactly what I saw. Calmly my sister then said, "It is the face of Christ." We were so very excited, of course, and my husband who had fallen asleep suddenly awoke and wanted to know why were excited. We then told him what we saw, but he couldn't see what we saw. I was very disappointed because I wanted him to enjoy the thrill of really seeing Christ's face.

Sudden the vision disappeared as suddenly as it had appeared.

I feel so greedy now, I wish to see him again. Please do not think this is the imagination of a silly woman. Both my sister and myself are middle aged women.

My main point in writing this letter to you Sir, is to tell you that Christ certainly watched over you during your trip into space.

From a Priest in Philadelphia

Amid the thousands of messages, you will receive, please accept this one. You will never know until eternity how many Catholic Priests, like myself, stood yesterday, in prayer at God's altar, for your safety—today at God's altar, in thanksgiving. *May He bless you, your family, parents and all dear to you.*

A Letter for my Mother

The world is full of worrying mothers. They pray that the Lord will take care of their children but they never completely believe that He will so they nullify their prayer. How often mothers send their children off with a "You know I'll worry every minute until you get home." If, instead they could take your example and believe as they pray in their hearts, "The Lord will bless you and keep you", then the world might produce many more Colonel Glenns.

From a Couple in Walnut Creek, California

Only peace with God will combat the sin of this world and as brothers and sisters in Christ we are all looking forward to the greatest space ride of all when we go to Heaven to live with the Lord.

"IS THERE A CEILING
TO THE SKY?"

CHAPTER 2

The questions that have been asked of me as a result of the flight have been as varied as imaginations can be, particularly where children are concerned. Many of these questions are good, well thought out, and show a considerable knowledge of the space program. Other questions are more humorous. Some, of course, get into areas having nothing at all to do with the space program. For some reason or another, being known in one special field persuades some people to make one an expert in other fields as well. This is obvious from some of the questions. I have added a few comments.

3/7/62

Dear Col. Glenn,

Is there a
ceiling to the sky? I
thought you could answer
this question because you
went up so high in the
rocket. I've always
wondered, because the
planes and jets go very
high, and looks as if the
is so high it will
never end. I saw your
trip on television and

From a Boy in Bucyrus, Kansas

I am writing you this letter because it is my assignment in English. If you would answere these I would be very grateful.

1. *What are your ideas on Education? Do you think all the work is worth it?*
2. *What do you think of girls sitting with boys on the way home from a basketball game? Do you think there is any harm in this? What do you think of dating in grade school?*

I am an eighth grader in Bucyrus, Kansas.

From an Eleven-Year-Old Boy in Presque Isle, Maine

I admire and envy you very much and I wish I could have made the trip with you. You could receive the glory as long as I could make the flight.

I have wondered about several things such as the yellowish green particles you reported and if any damage occurred to the capsule during re-entry without dropping the retropack. But the question I want to ask is what does the coast look like? Does the North American Continent look like it does on a map or does it have an entirely different shape.

From a Young Student

As a freshman student of South Catholic High School, I am studying Latin I. The question has arisen "What is the practical purpose of Latin?" As a man who has accomplished success in his goals I would ask you two questions: First, "Did you ever study Latin?" and if so, "what practical purpose in your life did it serve?"

My comment:

I refuse to answer on the grounds that what I say might tend to incriminate me with either 50,000 Latin teachers or 500,000 students, and in particular with Miss Barnett, my Latin teacher in New Concord High School.

From a Schoolgirl in Brooklyn, New York

You made all America very proud of you. It must be very interesting to have been in outer space and to show the world that this could be done. Could you answer these questions. Did you like your flight? If you can't take a person what 4 things would you take with you on the trip?

From an Eleven-Year-Old Californian

What happens if you are in a space helmet and your nose itches?

My comment:

Pure torture, believe me! But you'd be surprised at how adept one becomes at nose "wriggling" without having anything solid to rub against. Try it sometime.

From a First Grader in Haddonfield, New Jersey

Our first grade class is studying about space and about your ride in orbit. One big question to be answered is "What would happen to liquid soup if it was poured out in the capsule while in weightlessness?"

If you could find time we would be very interested in your answer.

My comment:

It would not pour because it is weightless, but if you did move the container and the soup came "floating" out, it would just keep moving in that same direction. Could get messy!

From a Schoolgirl in Niles, Illinois

If I went up into space I would feel wonderful, but yet lonely deep down inside. While you were up there did you pick a place to take a vacation?

25

From a Six-Year-Old Boy in Scarsdale, New York

I think you are wonderful for going to space. Can you come to my house for dinner next Friday?

From a Boy in Toronto, Canada

The first thing I'd like to say is, congratulations on your historical flight through space. I guess it gave you quite a thrill flying around the earth at that height and speed.

I would like to know a few things about your flight if you would not mind answering them. If you flew over Russia at that height would they have the right to shoot you down if they could?

From a Young Girl in Mantorville, Minnesota

My mother was in a car accident quite awhile ago or she would love to have writen to you.

I want to ask you some questions and I hope you answer them when you have time. I wrote another astronaut a letter but he didn't have time to answer my questions because he said he was busy.

1. Do you ever think in time that they will ever send women up in space?
2. Have you ever had any capsule that didn't land in water and and landed on the ground and if it did, could you use it over again?
3. If they ever ask you to go up again, would you do it?
4. When they send somebody up again will they try and go around the earth more than 3 times the next time? Do you know what I mean?
5. Did you have any pictures taken when you were going around the earth? If you did, will you send me some when you have time if they were any good.
6. Did you have a piece of that big cake? How much did it weigh and how high was it?
7. I bet it felt funny to go from night to day, didn't it?
8. Those clothes you put over your regular clothes, how much does it all weigh?

9. If anybody comes down that way on a trip, can they go through the plant.
10. Is Mr. Kennedy and his wife as nice to meet in person as he is on T. V?

I prayed all the time you was up there that you would come down safe and I guess my prayer was answered.

If I ever come down that way on a trip I'd love to meet all of the 7 Astronauts and their families.

My little brother wanted to stay home and watch you take off but he had to go to school so will you send him a couple pictures of you if you have any.

Will you have all the men write down there autograph for me please. My little brother would like that.

This is all I can think of so will close and hope you can answer my questions. when you have time and get the autographs from all of the astronauts and you.

My comment:

Now I know why the other astronaut said he was busy, but this shows the wonderful curiosity these young people have.

From a Girl in Milwaukee, Wisconsin

Today, in Church School we brought up the subject of Christians fighting in wars. Some men, as Christians feel that they should not kill, and they serve their country in some other way. But others feel that they should fight for Christianity. How do you feel about this? What do you think?

From a Nine-Year-Old Boy in Doylestown, Pennsylvania

I have been interested in space travel since I was six years old. I had special space maps that I studed hard. I got them from the world book encyclopedia.

I watched your space flight in school in which I was very much interested and also return trip. Are there any good books in the stores to help me be an Astronaut? Is there a test that you would spin in a chair at a great amount of speed? What colleges are good for training? Is it hard to be an astronaut?

I would like to be a astronaut because I think it would be exciting and I would like to help the United States to get to the planets.

2 West Broad Street
Paulsboro
New Jersey
August 7, 1962

Dear Colonel Glenn,
    Would it be possible if a
person went into space and
captured a star in a container?

              Yours truly,
              Dayla Ness

From a High-School Sophomore in Whiting, Iowa

I am a fifteen year old boy and a sophomore in high school. I need your advice. Ever since the launch of Sputnik I, I have read everything available on Space. I take four space magazines. I know that I want to be an astronaut. Should I join some branch of the service after graduation, like the U. S. Air Force Academy, or should I go to college and get hitched up with N.A.S.A.?

I wish to extend my highest congratulations to you and the many people that made your historic flight possible. Every morning that there was a possible launch I rolled out of bed at 4:00 A.M., but believe me it was worth it to finally get to watch that Atlas kick off the pad. At T-2 min. I was really excited. After that until about T-3 min. I sat spellbound in front of the T.V. I skipped school so I could watch your flight. So did a couple of my buddies. You're pretty popular with us but the Principal was beginning to have his doubts. Well, thanks a lot for your time and—be careful.

P.S. I get mostly A's and B's on my report card.

From a Young Boy in Ballstone Spa, New York

You are the bravest man I ever saw. I am in third grade. Was it fun to test your blood? You were lucky to have steak for breakfast. I am 8 years old.

My comment:
Blood, no—steak, yes.

From a Young Boy in West Upton, Massachusetts

I would like to have you answer a question that a person asked in school. I would like it very much if you could give an answer by the end of March. The question is if you had to go to the bathroom while you are in flight, what would you do? You may think that I am asking a silly question, but I would really like to know the answer because I think that it has a great deal to do with your space program.

My comment:

Seriously, this young man's question is a tough one for the engineers, too. It is a major problem area and a number of studies and tests have been and are being conducted, along with associated equipment development.

Flights to date have been short enough that we could cope with most of the problem by the use of low residue diets, but this will not do for longer duration missions.

From a Third-Grade Teacher in Ravenna, Ohio

The boys and girls in my third grade room wrote a story in our Language Class about, "What happened on February 20th, 1962." One little boy wrote, "Colonel Glenn carried the U. S. flag into space." This conjecture led to much discussion.

To my knowledge no statement had been made to that effect, altho' it seemed only the reasonable thing to assume.

I have listened to all the broadcasts on TV and Radio and also heard you relate the reverence which you have for the flag, but at no time has anyone definitely said there was a flag in the capsule.

Would you be kind enough to tell us if an American Flag did orbit the earth with you? And where will it's future home be, if so?

If it means anything to you, rest assured there is a little John Glenn Fan Club in my room who are gathering, reading, and listening to anything that is available about their Hero. You most certainly will never go out of their lives.

My comment:

There were five very small silk flags carried in a pocket of my suit. Their combined weight was not over one ounce. They were presented, one each, to: President Kennedy at the White House, the Commandant of the Marine Corps, the Smithsonian Institution, my daughter, Lyn, and son, Dave.

GLENN, GLEN
AND NEW GLENNS

CHAPTER 3

From a Tiny Baby in Pennsylvania
—Obviously Written by His Mother

Hi, I'm Johnny. My parents named me after you because I was conceived right around the time that you made your flight in "Friendship 7" (2/20/62). Also because my parents have a great interest in the space field.

From an Englishman

I am one of a large family of Glens and have just been looking at a picture of my Grandfather's brother, who went to America ages ago, he died in America round about 1934 and he used to spell his name with two n's.

From a Woman in Pennsylvania

May I tell you that my Great Grandmother's name was Glenn. And that is why I am writing you. To ask if you have any other Glenn names that I may trace for admittance into the D.A.R.

From a Physician in Illinois

We have joined the ranks of countless thousands of Americans who have named their son in your name in commemoration of such a memorial event. His name is Alan Glenn Manfredi.

From a Ten-Year-Old Boy in New York

The reason for my letter is that my mother had just had a baby on March 12, 1962. My father and mother agreed to name him John Glenn. We named him that because he was born at 3:00 which would stand for the 3 orbits that you went around the earth.

News Item:

Vernon—As American astronout Lt Col John Glenn zoomed out of this world last Tuesday, Maurice Stephen's milk cow was bringing two bull calves into the world.

When it came time to select names for the animals there was no problem.

You've guessed it . . . they were christened John and Glenn.

From a Religious School Group in Massachusetts

Please accept the enclosed Tree Certificate. This tree was planted in your honor in the Freedom Forest in Israel.

Birth Announcement from Canada

Announcing the launching of our new satellite
whose signals can be
heard all day
and throughout
most of the night

NAME OF MODEL: *John Glenn*
LAUNCHING DATE: *Sept. 29, 1962.*
WEIGHT IN SPACE: *7 lb. 4 oz.*
CHIEF ENGINEERS: *John and Glenna McKinley.*

From a Lady in Idaho

*The hose carts, of which there are two, are named "*FRIENDSHIP
NO. 1, *and* FRIENDSHIP NO. 2, *and have been in active service since
1887. This year will mark their 75th year of service to the small and
one time mining boom-townsite of Murray, Idaho.*

From a Woman in Minnesota

*Are you related to a ____? She tells me you are second cousin to
her, is that true or is ____ just throwing the bull?*

From a Mother in Ohio

Soon after your capsule went into orbit, I entered the hospital for
my fourth child—a hoped for little boy. His arrival coincided with
your safe recovery so we named him John Glenn Phillips.

From a Young Lady in Oregon

I have a hamster named John H. Glenn. H is for hamster.

From a Woman in California

"B-Decorated" racing for the first time under the new name of "Friendship 7 Stables" and with the new colors I designed in your honor.

From a School Principal in Nairobi, Africa

I cannot adequately express in words how grateful we are for your kind consent to let us name one of our school Boys' Houses after your illustrious name. We feel so honoured and elated at the privilege to associate our school with such a distinguished spaceman as you are.

From a Ten-Year-Old Boy in New Jersey

I thought that you were so great that you should be honored in my city. So I sent a petition to every one of our neighbors on my block that said that the street should be named John H. Glenn Ct. for 1 month. The mayor agreed and sent me the proclamation.

From a Vacationer in New York

Yes, we have named a forthcoming Lake after you. It just dawned on us that perhaps we should have written you first for your permission to do this.

From New York

ROAD NAMED FOR GLENN

Onondaga County paid tribute yesterday to astronaut Lt. Col. John H. Glenn, Jr.

By a resolution adopted at the Board of Supervisors meeting, a highway now under construction will be officially named John Glenn Blvd.

John Glenn Blvd., when completed in the near future, will run about 4 miles from Lakeland to Woodard Industrial Park, roughly parallel to the Long Branch Road.

From the President of a
Five-Member Boys Club in Florida

So now our club is called "THE JOHN H. GLENN MISSILAIRES CLUB"

From the Town Manager of South Windsor, Connecticut

". . . pay fitting remembrance of this great American by reserving as the name for the first park established in the Town, THE LT. COL. JOHN H. GLENN MEMORIAL PARK".

From a Church Group in Virginia

The first and sixth grade students of our Religious School made a contribution to plant two trees in Israel in your honor.

From the Dept. of Public Works of New York City

I wrote you March 21, 1962 in reference to sponsoring the new fireboat which is to be named in your honor.

From the Colorado Springs Gazette

Five sets of parents in Cleveland, Ohio, got into the act by naming their six newborn sons after the celebrated astronaut. Two were twins who divided the colonel's name.

If one had been a girl, the parents were no doubt prepared with something like Joanna Glenna.

One father noted that his wife "went into labor about the time Glenn went into orbit," the result bringing forth John Glenn Gonzales.

A check of Colorado Springs hospitals showed that several babies were born Feb. 20 but parents managed to refrain from honoring them in the Ohio way.

Finally, a call to the public information office of the Air Force Academy drew this jocular reply: "What! Name an Air Force baby after a Marine!"

From Cleveland, Ohio

Newspaper clipping:

FAMOUS NAMES, John and Glenn, were given to these twins born early yesterday to Mrs. Alice Vanni, 35, at St. Luke Hospital. The boys were expected to be but one child and arrived two weeks early at that, according to their mother. Father Roy and two other sons, 13 and 6 years, are waiting in their home at 9409 Bessemer Ave.

From a Mother in Washington

We couldn't name the baby John, as we already had a boy named Johnny, and didn't want to name him Glenn as a first name for fear the schools six years later would have such a crop of Glenns that the teachers would have to designate them as Glenn 1, Glenn 2, etc. So we used it as his middle name. He has the further distinction of being a unification of the Armed Forces baby, being a Navy baby (my husband was a Navy recruiter and a 20 year man) born in an Air Force Hospital (Fairchild) and named for a Marine! We couldn't manage to get the Army and the Coast Guard in on the act.

From a Young Girl in Ohio

Our dog had six pups, two boys and four girls. We named a boy in your favor, Glenn.

From a Family in California

"FROM OUT OF THIS WORLD"

JONNA GLYNN MORSE

SPECIFICATIONS:
Weight: 8 lbs. 1 oz.
Height: 21 inches
T-O: 10:50 A.M.
PROJECT ENGINEERS:
Sidney and Beverly Morse
"Mother and Child A—OK"

From a Young Boy

My family got a horse this week and we named him "John Glenn."

From a Father in Canada

During your experience I was lucky enough to have become the father of a son whom I have named, John Glenn, in your honor.

From a Woman in Oklahoma

In reading the Laughlin History again I learn that your Mother Jennie and my father Will Laughlin were double first cousins, isn't that interesting?

Woman from Arizona

My father was George Lincoln Glenn. We knew only those Glenn's who went from North Carolina to Illinois, and have always wondered about the others. All the Glenn's that I have known have been persons of good native ability and faithful to principle.

From an English Woman

I am anxious to know if you are a descendent of one of three young Glenns who emigrated to America in the 1860's from Horbling, Lincs. One of these boys was Henry Glenn, brother of my mother, Emma Glenn. The other two, George and Tom was her cousins. The former settled in Ohio and the latter at Stanford, Illinois.

It was the marked likeness of Col. Glenn to my relations which prompted me to write to you.

From a Woman in Delaware

I am enclosing a clipping from a newspaper which I received this morning from England. I thought perhaps you might be interested to read this, particularly if these people are your ancestors.

From an Elderly Irishwoman in New Jersey

If your people came over from the north of Ireland my Father had a sister married to a John Glenn near Mount Charles in the County Donegal.

From Ann Arbor, Michigan

You are the news of the day and they are too this week! I hope they grow as brave and good as you men.

3 AKC TOY POODLE PUPS "THE THREE ASTRONAUTS"

NAMES: *John Glenn*
Scott Carpenter
Walter Schirra
ARRIVED: *Mon. Oct. 29 3:00* A.M.
WEIGHT: *8 ozs. (?) Total*
PARENTS: AKC *"Miss Binini"* Reg.
"Jacques Astrojet-Hall"

From a Man in Florida

John and I may be "fourth cousins"!
My father's name was Frank S. Glen. My grandfathers name was William Henry Glen.

From a Woman in Minnesota

We think it was your grandfather who lived about five miles south of Cambridge. He and our mother were full cousins. So if he is your grandfather then we must be distant cousins and we are proud to be even distant relatives of so modest, brave and courageous a man.

My brother says he remembers of your grandfather taking him home with him from Cambridge and the first red pigs that he ever saw our father bought from your grandfather.

From a Woman in Wisconsin to my Mother

I watched with great pride your son on TV, glad that I am a Glenn and a Mackintosh (McIntosh).

Must tell you what my father used to say, you can always tell a Glenn they have nerves of steel.

From a High-School Teacher in Alabama to my Mother

Since we have the same family name I am wondering if we could be different branches of the same family. My relatives came from the Carolinas, and it has been rumored that the Glenn Family split, some of them coming southward and some of them going toward West Virginia and Ohio. I am related to a former federal judge of the Southern District of South Carolina named Glenn (first name unknown). Also one of my relatives was a doctor who came from South Carolina and settled in a north Georgia town (first name unknown also).

I would like to think that our branch of the family has the same untapped courage which was displayed by your son.

41

From a Greek Orthodox Pastor in Louisiana

On my desk I have two Greek News-Papers having your biography published, which reads as follows:

GLEN IS A 100 PERCENT GREEK
"When John grew up, took his Father name KLEANTHES, cut it short and instead KLEANTHES made it GLEN."

From a Woman in Maryland

I was told by some of my Hellenic friends of an article in a Greek-American newspaper that you, Colonel Glenn, are from Greek parentage on your father's side.

From a Woman in Alabama

My grandfather James Robert Glenn was killed at Missionary Ridge Chattanooga. His brothers were Gus, Walter, Thomas, Hersel, Bill and maybe John. His father was named John.

Please send this letter to your father to see if he knows this set of Glenn's.

My comment:

There was another "name" incident that showed a measure of ingenuity, to say the least. It was sent to me as a clipping from a magazine and related how three strip-tease performers had named themselves Alana Shepard, Gussie Grissom, and Jonnie Glenn. Their act was billed as being "out of this world."

IDEAS–PLAIN, FANCY, AND OUT OF THIS WORLD

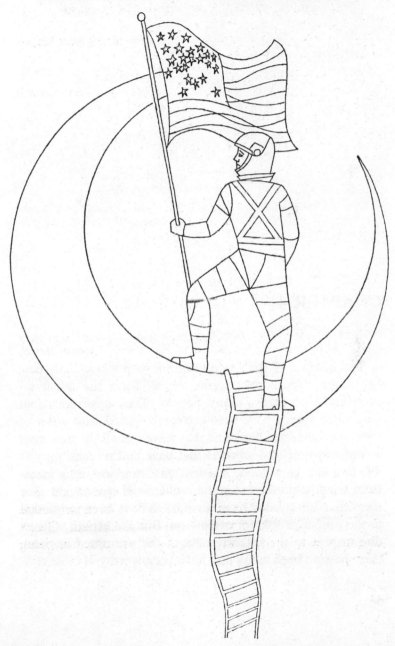

IDEAS FROM PEOPLE
NOT OF THIS WORLD

CHAPTER 4

The newness of the space program with its radically new engineering approaches seems to call forth the latent inventiveness of many, many people. The suggestions that have been offered have been extremely varied. Just a few of them are submitted here, and they have run all the way from completely crackpot schemes that have had no feasibility at all, to some very good, learned, and practical suggestions from scientists interested in the problems of space flight. The ideas that appeared to have some merit have been forwarded to the proper people for evaluation. But I'm afraid, with all due respect to the inventiveness of the average American, there haven't been many that have been worthy of close consideration. For the most part, a high percentage of the letters suggesting ideas seek to apply a single concept into a completely different field. As an example, I think the suggestions regarding the use of atomic power have received more thought from more people than any other single idea. They could not understand why we still use old-style boosters with rocket fuel and hard-to-handle liquid oxygen when we could very simply use atomic energy to do the same job. The formidable complexities of applying atomic power to space flight don't seem to faze them at all.

In a way, I guess, this is typically American, for we are completely free to present any idea on any subject to anyone.

From a Girl in Montrose, Missouri

Could those particles have been from the lost Milky Way?

From a Man in New York

When Commander Shepard made his historic flight TIME printed a facsimile of the N.A.S.A. Distinguished Service Medal he received and later that you also received. TIME commented that it looked like something out of a crackerjack box. I agreed and just recently had time to think about it, and I felt you and your fellow-astronauts deserved something more appropriate for the occasion. So I sketched a couple of designs more in keeping for the event.

From Another Man in New York

I saw you on television in orbit around the Earth in 1962, and set out to invent a toy to compliment you.

It is the object of my invention to simulate in toy form, the orbiting of a space satellite around the Earth, and the tracking of this satellite by means of a radar beam.

I call this toy the Earth Satellite Radar Tracking Station, and I would like it to be for rememberance of you in admiration.

From a Chairman of the Board

Noticed a newspaper clipping where you are using a slingshot for survival purposes. Would you have an interest in one that is considerably better than any I have ever seen?

There is quite a story about slingshots I have made over the years from surgical rubber. I have no trouble shooting with 5⁄8″ ball bearings through 3⁄8″ of hardwood plywood.

Would be glad to furnish you one upon request if you will give me a report on its effectiveness.

We also make Marble Survival Knives and own Marble Arms who were makers of fine knives for 75 years.

A Young Lady in Washington, D. C., Writes:

The Soviets have sent at least six astronauts into orbit around the earth, losing them out there, still orbiting around the world, after the Russians lost control of them.

It seems to me that the United States could track one of these abandoned space vehicles, timing the capsule's revolutions, and send, either a manned rocket or remote controlled missile up after it, equipped with an electro magnet to snatch the Soviet's dead astronaut and ship back to the United States for observation and propaganda reasons. Is this possible to accomplish?

3000
MICHIGAN 2-3001
3002

WURTH ELECTRIC MOTOR CO.

Motors, Generators, Alternators • Frequency Changers

Generator Sets Built to Your Specifications
REPAIR, REWIND, REDESIGN EXPERTLY

75-20 Jamaica Ave. • Woodhaven 21, N. Y.
P. O. BOX 1131   February 27, 1962

Lt. Col. John H. Glenn, Jr. & Fellow Astronauts
c/o White House
Washington, D. C.

Gentlemen:

Below are sketches of a device or devices of food containers to
dispense liquid or food paste at zero gravity. Figure 1 show's a
food container with a flexible balloon like device on one end, a
sliding disk between food chamber and balloon; food is filled in
and then compressed air or oxygen is filled in at nozzle on balloon
cap. Unit is now ready for operation by inserting mouthpiece into
the mouth, food nozzle is opened and compressed air will force food
into the mouth of its operater at will.

Continued on page 2.

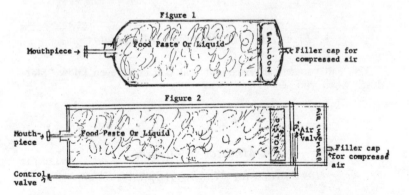

Figure 1

Figure 2

From a Grandmother in Los Angeles

Perhaps I can account for your "Glenn Effect" particles. As you no doubt recall, the vapor particles you saw were white, but because you undoubtedly stared a long while at the orange-red sunrise, then glanced at the white vapor against a gray background, the color complementary to red appeared as a green after-image, and colored the particles green. I hope this simple explanation is the true one. I had a similar experience years ago.

After a long monotonous day of desert driving, I was somewhat shaken to find as dusk approached, that all the oncoming cars had green headlights! As I was driving due west into a blinding red sunset, the white headlights only appeared to be green. I had had a few courses in Psychology at U.C.L.A. and decided the effect could only be explained as a negative after-image. I thought the fact that you observed the green particles only at sunrise—probably a brilliant one—undoubtedly gave color to otherwise white vapor. It would explain why you couldn't photograph color which existed only as a psychological visual sensation.

P.S. If this explanation is accepted as the true one, my grandsons are certainly going to be amazed.

From a Girl in Pine City, Minnesota

You call yourself an astronaut and you don't even know "Stardust" when you see it.

A Minister in Oregon
Has an Idea for Making Airplanes Safer

My improvement idea is to have two or three small helicopter propellers on top of the plane. If anything happened to the regular engines of the plane the Helicopter propellers could be put into position and motion thus bringing the plane down to earth in slow motion.

From a Seventy-Four-Year-Old Australian

In your account of your wonderful journey in orbiting the earth the mystery "Fireflies" described by you sent my memory back forty years to 1922 or 1923 when I had a somewhat similar experience, only I was right down here on earth.

I watched the sparks for a while as they were still raining from over the back of my house twelve to fifteen feet or so high. The sparks glowed . . .

I thought at the time that it was some kind of an electrical disturbance. There was no rain, lightning or thunder at the time. I have never seen fireflies, and I don't think we have any in Victoria.

I can remember when I was a child probably about six years old living in Melbourne and some people were talking about a rain of stars. I vaguely remember them saying that this would be repeated at some future time . . .

From a Physician in New Hampshire

Perhaps the following suggestion is entirely naive, however, it seems reasonable enough to me that I am sending it along for your consideration on the matter of capsule attitude controls.

The suggestion is that the capsule magnetic field voluntarily be altered by zonal wiring and variable current flow to take advantage of this phenomenon providing an internal electrical means of aligning and stabilizing the capsule.

If it can be done with a free floating compass needle, why not a capsule or satellite?

From a Man in Florida

May I submit for your consideration, a possible technical explanation for the "fireflies" which have been observed by you, Mr. Titov, and Commander Carpenter during orbital flights.

I believe this is a phenomenon which is due to the naturally occurring fluorescent or phosphorescent characteristics of interplanetary dust present in space. This is the same material which is credited with the astronomical phenomenon known as "zodiacal light."

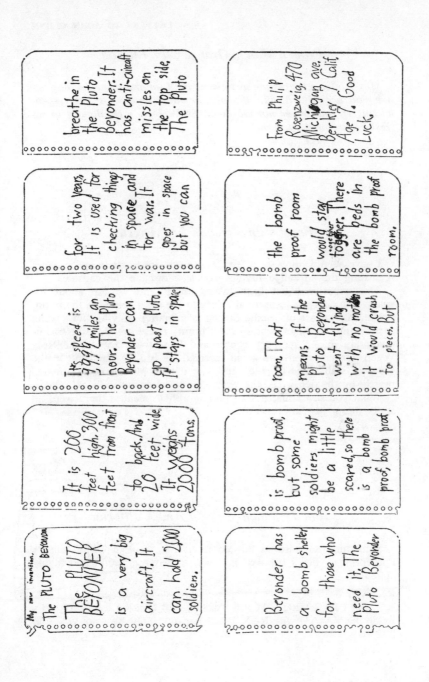

My new invention. The PLUTO BEYONDER

The PLUTO BEYONDER is a very big aircraft. It can hold 2000 soldiers.

It is 260 feet high. 300 feet from front to back. And 20 feet wide. It weighs 2,000 tons.

Its speed is 7999 miles an hour. The Pluto Beyonder can go past Pluto. It stays in space

for two years. It is used for checking things in space, and for war. It goes in space but you can

breathe in the Pluto Beyonder. It has anti-aircraft missiles on the top side. The Pluto

Beyonder has a bomb shelter for those who need it. The Pluto Beyonder

is bomb proof, but some soldiers might be a little scared, so there is a bomb proof, bomb proof

room. That means if the Pluto Beyonder went flying with no motors it would crash to pieces. But

the bomb proof room would stay together. There are beds in the bomb proof room.

From Philip Rosenzweig. 470 Michigan ave. Berkley 7 Calif. Age 7. Good Luck.

From a Man in Orange City, Florida

May I offer a suggestion as to what the Luminous Specks may be! Are you acquainted with the phenomenon known as the Gegenschein? If you are or not look it up in Webster's Dictionary to refresh your memory.

From a Physician in Los Angeles

I have been waiting for a few days to see some article in the paper regarding the so called fireflies you saw outside the capsule.

This experience has been talked about and written about for years. The cause is an unusual injury to the sight center in the brain, similar to the act of seeing. Seeing is a matter of vibrations being carried into the sight center of the brain. These are transferred immediately into a memory center and kept there for further use. When like vibrations are again received we project them out in the form of sight. The distance and size of the objects are estimated mostly by the density of the vibrations received by the sight center.

What you saw could not be photographed because there were no spots there, just impressions.

From a Woman in Santa Ana, California

Something so unusual has come to me through Extra-Sensory Perception. When I received it, I was told it was secret and highly classified.

Received 8-29-62:
KO/YO LIO Set 202 X11 P 6 Velocity 320 Use the LA X 21 RAX Begin the VA/631 with RAX 296 Other set 10/20 XIV not GN ZZZ 202

From a Chef in Ohio

The recipe for my "Astronaut."

I am happy to report the "Astronaut" was featured on our Sunday menu recently and met with great success.

If you are ever in this vicinty, I would be happy to have you as our guest, and prepare the "Astronaut" for you.

From a Lady in Dillon, South Carolina

Not being a scientist, I am not confounded by the complexities of modern rocketry.

I am wondering why you cannot use a pumping system on rocket's rear. A constant pumping pressure action could keep the rocket going just as far and as long as wished. It might mean even a lighter rocket could be used as once weightlessness is reached, the constant pumping pressure would keep it climbing. It might save fuel, too. This would be a combination of two principles—motor-pulling and pump-pushing forces.

From a Man in Tarzana, California

The thought occurred to me, that a shield in the form of a cone helix might be used to retard the speed of your return.

Some time ago I learned this principle from mother nature. After observing the different methods of trees in spreading their seeds away from the close proximity of the tree, I became interested in the pine cone. As it opened up the pine cone became a cone helix thereby allowing the wind to carry it away from the tree. I made models of the cone helix and by experimenting found out by closing the top of the spiral, I retarded the air going thru and obtained a lift. I found out that the open top cone helix was a moulded path that a propeller cuts in turning.

From a Young Man in Johnson City, Tennessee

I have invented a piece of playground equipment that creates more excitement among the teenagers in recreation centers than anything since you went into orbit.

The manager of the park and recreation center here thinks this unit has a wonderful potential with proper promotion.

I am enclosing a photograph so you can see what it looks like. I was in a revolving motion when this picture was taken. A slight up and down movement of the body rotates it, and exercises most all your muscels. They could be made in different sizes for different age groups.

From a Man in California

I have a small idea I thought might help and would like to pass it on to you.

To coat or even integrate a luminous chemical or paint into or onto the outer casing of the capsule would make it visible in the night sky. A night launching would be far more easily observed than a daytime launching as there would be no refraction of light to hamper viewing, also the sky is more apt to be clear midway between the setting and the rising of the sun than at those specific times.

From a Man in Riverside, California

I have an idea on an Atomic Powered Device (or whatever you may call it)—a way to take moon trips without worrying about the blast-off of a Rocket.

The thrust in today's Rockets wreck all of the delicate wiring. My idea eliminates this terrible shock on take-off.

Where shall I send my idea.

If we are to beat the Russians, at least, my idea is worth listening to.

From a Man in California

Inventor —— didn't want you to fly my satalitte airoplane, I have notified police to cancel out flite. and all so you whent against my say so and stold my satallitte airoplane and Mr. President Kennedy in a thief like your kind, and people of United States all so are crime. I want you senced to prisons over this.

From a Woman in San Francisco

I have three years law knowledge, 7-years of electronics & engineering & drafting. I have plans for a Flying Saucer.

I would like to take a part in the Space Age. Please state how I might go about this.

From a Man in Philadelphia

In making coffee in a glass coffee maker I notice that if I toss a spoonfull of powdered coffee and/or sugar into the utensil I get an instant reaction of foam which rises and bubbles over the top.

Could this be of some value in boosting the energy of a secondary jet?

From a Yorkshireman

I went to see your space cone in London. I was very impressed by it, and I still think you need an extra shell on the major walls for protection.

SECOND LETTER:

I am writing again, to ask if you are receiving my letters safe.

I suggested that a thin outer shell around the major walls of the spaceship would insulate it from the sound, and it might also protect the wall itself from dents or holes that some of the meteors punch into it.

AROUND THE WORLD

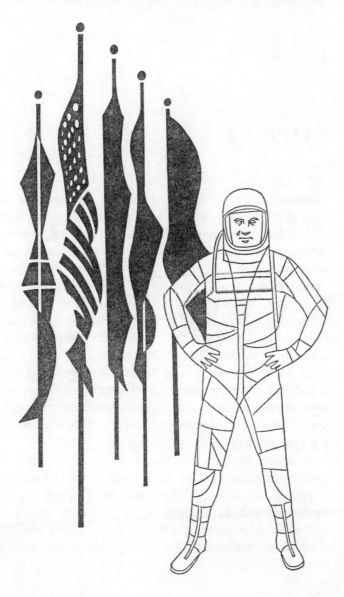

CHAPTER 5

Most of the mail received from international sources around the world was much the same as that received from within the United States. There were, however, some notable differences. ". . . proves the tremendous national power of USA produced by the peoples . . ." The man who wrote those words was a Captain in the Japanese Navy and he was concerned. He was kindly concerned that we had finally made the orbital flight a success, wanted to express his thanks, and finished with the sentence "May our firm unity overwhelm the invasion of Communists."

Many of the letters from foreigners mentioned using our capabilities in space for peaceful means, and there was concern expressed, too, that atomic bombs not be placed in space. Most of the letters received from Russia and the Iron Curtain countries were very friendly in nature.

It is also obvious that many people in foreign countries look to America and all Americans as a land of riches and a people of plenty. There have been many requests for money as well as requests to aid students, young people, and some older people to come to this country. Most of these we referred to authorities who might be able to help in some way.

A Young Girl from London, England, Writes:

I heard on the telivision that there may be a man on the moon by 1970 and if you want to I hope you are given the opportunity to go.

If you wanted to blow your nose or you sneezed what would you do and could you take your helmet off.

A Twelve-Year-Old Boy from
Northumberland, England, Writes:

We call you "John The Lionheart" because that is what our English Kings are called when they are very brave and we think you are even braver than they were. They only had swords and things to be afraid of.

From a Man in Modena, Italy (as translated)

To your dear little girls, your Mother, your great and noble Father I wish from all my heart many, many happy years and glorious new ventures for the good of all humanity!

Long Live America
Long live your President
Long live Italy and all the brothers of the World

From a Foreign Exchange Student from The Netherlands

I held my breath about every minute of the count down, afraid that something might delay the launching. Then finally we saw you take off from Cape Canaveral and I want to tell you that at that moment I did not feel Dutch, but I felt completely like an American that was really one of the most wonderful moments in my life.

59

From a Greek in Athens

We Greek people are very proud of wonderful success, and may God give you power for greater Sucsess. I am a Greek by birth I am shure you know we Greek people are the best friends you have in America. We always were and we will always be.

Anything you would like to send you from Greece write and let me know please I would be more than glad to send it. Such as a beautiful imbroided table cloth with napkins as Greece is noted for Imbroidery you know we have some of the worlds best imbroidery, or perhaps a beautiful set of scales in brass carved very beautifully called the Scales of Justice, a Doll of the Greek Island Costtom, anything you like tell me in your letter I would be pleased to send it to you. And I also have several Greek Bizantine Empire coins that are still in perfect shape if someone may like:

And if you please can do me a favor honorble friends. If you could inclose in your letter $20 so as i could buy myself a suiet of clothes that I am badly in need off.

To David Glenn from a Filipino Girl

Well I'll introduce my self and hobbies. My full name is Naomi Ruth Gazo Paspe, pure Pilipina with brown complexion, has long black hair, regular in height, small eyes and mouth, short nose and a daughter of both teacher. My mother and father are both Pilipino and they are both teacher. I'm studing in Naburaturan Provincial High School and I'm 14 years in old, born on May 9, 1948. My hobbies are playing piano, playing cards, writing, reading, telling funny stories, cooking and most of all I spend my leisure time in going to the church.

Society I seldom go with them, but instead I spend my time by reading much of Dr. Jose Rizal who is our national hero and Perry Mason's pocket book and reading Bible.

Going to parties and movies I spend my time in the church singing and reading Bible. Record and disrecord, well I'm singer I like to heard songs from Pat Boome, Elvis Presley, Johnny Mathis, and especially all songs of Paul Anka, and plays its record. Well this all I can say about my self and hobbies, I hope you enjoy reading my letter.

From a Boy in Jerusalem

I admire your flight to the space and I wish you great success in your research work. We hope that all your work will be of great help to the establishment of world's peace.

We children of Israel, pray together with the children of the whole world to live happy and healthy life, and to enlarge our knowledge from your achievements.

From a Man in Middlesex, England

As a Britisher I feel I voice the re-actions of all British people when I say simply "Sincere congratulations on your wonderful achievement, and more so, thank God for your safe return."

Maybe you might have received many of the enclosed cuttings, but just in case you have not I enclose what I feel is too much of a co-incidence. Cannot help feeling that John Glenn of Cornwall, England, was trying to catch up to you, and on the same day.

Newspaper clipping enclosed.

ANOTHER SPEEDY GLENN

John Glenn, of Carbis Bay, was fined £3 by West Penwith, Penzance magistrate's court, for speeding—at 52 m.p.h.

A High-School Student from Pütsstr, Germany, Writes:

I am genuine. I am no a spy for the east or to the sowjets. I hate the Kommunismus, but like the Kapitalismus, the blue Army, the West, especially the U. S. A. and Germany.

A Foreign Exchange Student
from Hjörring, Denmark, Writes:

I know that as well Denmark as the rest of Europe follows the progress in American Science and especially now, the mercury project Because we know that if it should come to a III World War, which we really don't believe in, a little state as Denmark could do nothing against a big power as i.e. the Russians. Therefore almost every Dane is very enthusiastic about the space program, and not least about the man who goes up.

To Lyn from a Filipino Girl

First of all I will let you know about myself. I'm 14 years old and a Junior student of Cebu Institute of Technology. I like the movies, writing, going to church and wading.

Lyn, I would try to ask you, what did you feel when you come to know that your father was on journey? Did you say some prayers? How about your mother? What was the reaction of your brother?

To David Glenn from a Schoolboy
in Villanueva del Arzobispo, Spain

Don't be surprised that I call you my friend when we have never seen each other; the point is that I think all young people in the world ought to be friends. That is what I and my 350 schoolmates think. And so we have agreed to send you this letter. We want to be your friends, among other reasons because you have a father who is such a brave tio *(literally, uncle) and does those things that everybody now knows.*

We have also agreed to invite you to pass a few days with us. For your father who knows how to rise to such heights and who makes so many turns around the earth in such a short time, it will not be very hard to put you in a plane and in one hop—zas!—take you to Spain where we await you with open arms. We really hope you come and you will see what a good time we have. Although this is a school for poor children, we have a very beautiful garden, we run around the paths but without injuring the flowers and plants; we have a playing field where we take part in many sports and have gymnastics; the teachers like us and teach us many things—also about the United States.

Oh! I forgot to tell you to please bring a large photograph signed by your father. We will put it alongside that of our Christopher Columbus, who was another tio *as big as he.*

Let us know when you are coming so we can meet you.

To Mrs. Glenn from a Woman in Southern Rhodesia

We had your husband's wonderful achievement on our T.V. programmes out here in Africa, and they broadcasted on the wireless a direct link with America of the actual take off—while the count down was in progress I was walking round my garden praying so much for you and your family but especially for you. Being a wife and mother like you I could put myself in your place and know just how you were feeling, knowing that your man was going up into the unknown. You were the bravest of the lot and I salute you.

As I sit writing to you I look out of the window and can see the country and the sun is shining and I can hear the little wild birds singing who I feed every day and it makes me realize what a lovely world we live in. Its a good world to fight for and a good world to give all we have got to make the world a better place for everyone.

God's Richest Blessings on you and yours.

To Lyn Glenn from a Boy in Indonesia

With this piece of paper I want to make my acquaintance with you. My name is Andi Nurr. I'm 19 years old. I attend a High School at 12th grade.

I read some magazines and newspapers who told about your father as a famous man in the world. So I know everything about him as the astronaut. I saw you and your mother and your brother David in the picture of the magazine.

So if you don't mind, I want to be your pen pal. I hope you like to tell me about you, maybe about your school, your friend, your father, mother, etc. So maybe you can tell me about your hobby. I like your father. My hobby is: riding two horses, swimming, skiing water, dancing, singing, climbing a mountain, collecting stamps, money etc.

I hope you'll be glad to receive this letter and you don't mind to answer.

Salatiga, January 12, 1963.

Dear Miss Carolyn,
With this piece of paper I want to make
my acquaintance with you. My name is
Andi Num. I'm 19 years old. I attend a
High School. at 12th grade.
I read some magazines and newspapers who
told about your father as a famous man
in the world. So I know everything about
him as the astronaut, I saw you and
your mother and your brother David in
the picture of the magazine.
So if you don't mind, I want to be
your pen pal. I hope you like to tell
me about you. maybe about your school,
your friend, your father, mother etc,
So maybe you can tell me about your hobby.
I like your father? My hobby is:
riding a horse, swimming, sking water,
dancing, singing, climbing a mountain
collecting stamps, money etc
I hope you'll be glad to receive this letter.
and don't mind to answer
         you
I'm sorry my English is too bad, but I
like to learn better
         So long   Your sincerely
                          Andi Num

From a Publisher in Assen, The Netherlands

Before you start, I, as a publisher of a very small Dutch daily, would like to ask you for a favour. Will you please carry on your body one sheet of our daily while you are doing your fantastic journey? And send it back to me afterwards with your autographed photo? This will enable me to publish that we were the first daily out in space.

Salutation from an Irish Family

Radio relay of your unique flight brought great pleasure here in Ireland. Your voice came through so clear and relaxed. Lights flashed in Perth, Aus. and in our Irish home. Our Blessed Candle gently glowed on our small living room altar. Our petition to Mary, God's Mother for your well being and safe return. You have replaced Fairy mythology in our children's day dreams, and done your country proud honour. God Bless you.

From a Schoolgirl in Sussex, England

This is just a postcard to say congratulations. It was our English teacher who told us that you had taken off successfully and we spent the lesson talking about space, moons, astronauts, etc. Anyone who helps to waste my school time is a hero of mine, whether he's been three times around the world or not. You don't know me, I'm an English girl, but once again, congratulations.

From a Man in Brisbane, Australia

My prayers were with you Sir. My little six year old daughter forgot everyone, in her bedtime prayers, including me, and dedicated them entirely to you.

Now Sir, It comes to us Australians that the question has been put to you, that perhaps it is a waste of public money to train the astronauts to such an extent. In view of that I am prepared to offer my services (do or die) as a man of limited training in a manned space program.

Sir, there is no backing out, I was one who laughed at the early talks of manned space, and STILL refuse to believe that the Russians 'got' there, that their whole operation was for properganda. But now that I have been proved wrong I would like to dedicate any thing I can towards it, and all I can offer is my life.

By God above, I take this solemn oath that what I have offered, as above, I pledge to fullfill, if I am called upon.

A Student from Ter Aar, The Netherlands, Writes:

I ask you if you will write this article about the person of President John Kennedy with regard to the project of the travelling in space. I very hope that you will do it.

From a U.S. Army Wife in Istanbul, Turkey, Relayed via Time Magazine

Living so close to Russia puts great significance on your achievement.

The islamic people of Turkey are observing Ramadan, which is a thirty day period of fasting and Prayer. I am sure that many prayers were said even in islamic, for your safe return.

From a Man in Tarragona, Spain

I never had any doubts that the U.S. would find its deserved place in aviation. In this, time helped and of course so did you. It really cheered up this old refugee of the first world war.

I heartily congratulate you on your successful flight, I embrace you and your children, and your wife; I press your hand and I wish you happiness in your further work for your homeland and humanity.

If you remember me sometime, come visit me if you are in Spain. If I'm alive, I'll embrace you, if I'm dead, look in the cemetery— Cemeterio Sta Tesla, S^{an} Lazaro No. 367.

High-School Students from Hof Saale, Germany, Write:

Your success is the classical example of teamwork. We can affirm you that the German people shares in the admiration of all the world.

As our passions are the technical constitutions of the rockets and we are admiring every success of the United States, we write to you.

From a Nigerian Chief

Though somewhat belated, it may not be out of place for me, a Chief of Kalabari in the Rivers Province of Eastern Nigeria and an ex-Member of Parliament, to add a personal note to the millions of congratulations you no doubt have received on your successful space flight over the Earth.

My peculiar position in this wonderful event is the impression which the marvelous space ship 'Friendship 7' you used has given me, an instrument which I and thousands of Nigerians viewed at Lagos recently—a practical demonstration of American scientific supremacy.

I pray, as you have done, that Almighty God may direct that such scientific discoveries as the space achievement may result in greater good to mankind.

Washington, D.C., August " 16 ", 1962.

Dear Lieutenant-colonel Glenn,

The Embassy was requested by Soviet citizen Mr. Podyr-zev (Voronesh, USSR) to obtain some stamps issued in the United States in honor of you and other American austronauts with your personal autograph. The stamps will be showed at a children exhibition.

I would appreciate very much if you could sign the envelopes enclosed herewith.

In accordance with the request of Mr. Podyrzev I am sending you herewith the stamps issued in the Soviet Union in honor of the Soviet cosmonauts which Mr. Podyrzev's son would be glad to présent to you.

Sincerely yours,

Anatoly F. Dobrynin
Ambassador

From a Young Boy in La Spezia, Italy

So you, pioneer of cosmos, let me, little Italian boy, express you all my infinite admiration for your achievement which rise to a heroic meening, and please, satisfy, if you can, my very desire: I wish I could have a picture of yours mailed with the special stamp issued in U.S.A. to celebrate the important day that made of you a National Hero of the most emancipated and democratic Nation in the world.

It will be, besides an ardently desired present, the most singular and appreciated piece in my philatelic collection, that I'm building up with my papa's help.

It might be that my desire is too indelicate and presumptuous, but I wish you'll forgive me, 'couse I know that you love children, in each one you see the needs and wishes of your David and Lyn. Kiss them for me and for all Italian children.

Anyway, please accept my best wishes for you, your family and for all your next victories which the Lord appointed you for.

Yours with much love

P.S. To make it easier for you, I asked a friend of mine to translate this letter in English, a language that I will study as soon as I'm big enough to go to school and learn Languages.

From a Man in Belgium

Coming back in VIELSALM after two months of holidays, I find your wonderful letter in which you accept to become the Honorary President of our Club named FRIENDSHIP VIII in honor of your wonderful exploit in your space capsule FRIENDSHIP VII. (The purpose of our club—as I wrote it—is to help mentally and physically handicapped children in our area to go to school who up until now have not been accepted in any schools) and your picture.

Let me thank you very, VERY MUCH for both. Having such a glorious Honorary President will help us in making money for our little friends in a great deal.

Do not forget that should you come to my country—where the American soldiers gave so generously their blood during the BATTLE OF THE BULGE—that you will have a home.

From a Boy in Sunyani, Ghana

John, I am sixteen and a half year old, and I am happy about Science, so I can offer myself if your country needs somebody to do the same as you did. I will be glad if you will send me science books to read.

Glenn, how I love you, only God knows even you cannot know. I always pray for you so that God may give you and your family long life and our friendship to be strengthened.

I know, before I become Twenty years, (20yrs) you will try to help me to come to you at America, and by all means I will come to you before I die. I think you like Ghanaians things. Our most beautiful thing in Ghana is our own rich cloth call "KENTE". The one you see most important Ghanaians put it on when they go to Untied Nations. I shall have you one when you visit Ghana. The cost is very dear but because I love you, I will try my best.

From a Child in Novosibirsk, U.S.S.R.

Third Cosmonaut, Col. John Glenn, for his daughter:

I, Olga, send you my warmest pioneer greetings. I congratulate you and all of your country for the great scientific achievement of accomplishing a space flight with a man on board. Really it is very good that on our planet, 3 men have become cosmonauts: Yurily Alekseyevich Gagarin, Ghermann Stepanovich Titov, and your father. When peace makes its advent, all of us together will achieve much more. You are probably very proud that it was your father who became the third astronaut. If you wish, we will correspond with one another. Probably you don't know Russian, just as I don't know English. Never mind, write to me in English, they can translate it here. I am an 8th class student in the N34 intermediate school in the city of Novosibirsk. Please write and tell me what you do, where you are studying, in general everything. Where does your mother work? What is your weather like? If you wish, your brother

71

can write to the boys in our class. In general, what do you think of us, the Russians? Are you envious that we are building communism? Who knows, perhaps we can become lifelong friends.

Au revoir. Say hello to your father, your brother and your mother.

I am 14 years old too. I also have a brother Nicky, but he's 2 years my junior. He's in the 6th class. My mother's name is Nina. I have no father.

From a Uruguayan Boy Living in Connecticut

I want to express my admiration for your wonderful feat, not only my feeling but the feeling of the Uruguayan people who send you their love and admiration because this what you have done is an historic event and nobody will forget your name and what you have done for the Science and for the Humanity.

A Seventeen-Year-Old Boy from
Jacob Jong, The Netherlands, Writes:

In my bedroom hang colour photographs of David and Lyn. What is Lyn a beautiful girl. Real! Ask her to write to me (in Englisch, Dutch or German). Say her: I have the height of you (1.80 meter), blue eys, 17 year, birth on October 25, 1945, I am by the Revormed Church (De Gereformeerde Kerken van Nederland), I am on a higher-grade school in the 4 classe, my father is 51, my mother 49 years old. I have 2 brothers and 4 sisters.

Say her, that she have a beautiful green waistcoat and a jolly petticoat on my big photograph.

From a Man in Cracow, Poland

I was very pleased to get your letter informing me that your to get the book of Cracow. I am sorry to say: during all the time of war I was in concentration lager in Germany to day I am patiens! Rheumatic, momentary blindness and having no presence of mind! I am cannot to work hard! What am I to do? My income is no more than 300 dollars on year! terrible! that won't do for me! For God's sake—I am to die of hunger with my family: wife and two son's. I hope you'll excuse me! To present me please 200/two hundret/dollars—only once on year! No more! May I aks you to do it? Would you mind? I should really very grateful to you! I don't know what should have done without your help!

All the best wishes to your noble President. God bless you all. Waiting for you ansver.

From a Former Political Prisoner Now Living in Chicago

I am an American citizen who, at the age of 19, was sentenced to 18 years in prison by the Red regime in Czechoslovakia on charges of espionage. Although I was innocent, I spent 13 years in Communist prisons until my release this May. I owe my freedom to the pressure exerted by American organizations and unknown friends in the United States.

Now that I am living in this free land, I wish to express my greatest admiration for your daring orbit into space and to thank you for raising by your flight the spirit of the political prisoners behind the Iron Curtain and their faith in the United States.

It may interest you that as soon as the news of your orbit became known in prison, tens of prisoners came to me to voice their joy over your success. They look upon it as an American victory

73

in the race with the Soviets and I, as an American, was congratulated for this triumph.

I would be very happy if you could assure your colleagues-astronauts that their success is followed closely by people behind the Iron Curtain and that they are greatly strengthened in spirit by your feats.

From a History Teacher in the U.S.S.R.

On this day of the commemoration of victory over Germany, permit me to congratulate you, the American cosmonaut, and to wish you the best of success in your activity. Our cosmonaut, G. S. Titov, having circled the globe 17 times, visited you in America. Titov's visit will undoubtedly strengthen the friendship of the Soviet and American peoples. As concerns us, the Soviet people, we will remember the period of the grim war from 1941–1945. The joint friendship of the people of the USSR and of the USA aided us to be victorious in 1945. Then, in the meeting at the Elbe River, the Soviet and the American soldiers shook hands. It would be desirable for this friendship to be preserved now, when the awesome nuclear weapon of destruction exists in the world. Let me wish you from the bottom of my heart the best of luck in your work, and congratulations on your victory in the cosmos.

From a Man in Pretoria, South Africa

Not one of the lesser pleasures derived from your flight for the Free World is the knowledge that Soviet Russia is no longer so far ahead in the Space Race. Uncle Sam can look Mr. K. right into the face and tell him that he, Sam, can do it too. Speaking about Russia, it would appear that they can suffer as many failures as they like—maybe they do—because they tell us only of the successful attempts. In a democratic country like the States, however, where the human life is still the most important factor, the whole world knows about its failures as well as its successes and this makes the success of your flight to us so much more wonderful. As one newspaper put it—"Gagarin rode up there alone, but Glenn took the whole world along for the ride."

From a Priest in Balatonszabadi, Hungary

I confess Yon, beside the pure and sincere congratulation, the writing of my letter has another purpose.

I myself should congratulate you with the most unselfish enthusiasm, but I am the priest of a small village which have suffered much in the war. The village is near the beautiful lake Balaton.

The tower of our church was consumed by fire in the war and it is now also in demolished state, because the acquisition of money is a great care for us. We want now to begin the restoration of the original top of the tower. We beg also your help to this great work.

We should perpetuate with pleasure your name and the date and the circumstances of your excellent achievement with your outogram, placed in the globe under the cross.

From a Man in Lipetsk, U.S.S.R.

As with all Soviet people, I was sincerely delighted by the successes which were attained by the American people in the peaceful conquest of outer space. Your name and the names of your friends, Allen Shephard, Gus Grissom, Scott Carpenter, and Gordon Cooper, as well as the names of our cosmonauts Yuri Gagarin, German Titov, Andrian Nikolayev, Valeriy Bykovskiy, and Valentina Tereshkova, became a symbol of courage, valor, and heroism. Your flights serve the cause of knowledge of the world which surrounds us in the name of the happiness of man and peace on earth.

I am very glad that your government signed the treaty banning the test of nuclear weapons under water, in the atmosphere, and in outer space, which makes safe the flights of man in space. I hope that you will rise into space many times.

From a Man in Omsk, U.S.S.R.
as Received from the Translator

The writer congratulates Col. Glenn on his successful space flight. He is married and is the father of a daughter and a son. The son was born at 9:00 A.M. on February 20, Omsk time. The writer has decided to name his son John in honor of Col. Glenn (in Russian it will be "Dzhon"). He hopes that his children will grow up in an era when airports are no longer built, with space-ports replacing them. He also hopes that the next cosmonaut who flies into space will find a corner where all nuclear weapons may be scrapped permanently. He hopes that his children will be able to see the beauty of the earth from space. Up to now only "three fine fellows" have seen this beauty, which is like that of a blushing bride's face surrounded by flowers. The writer would like to receive a reply from Col. Glenn.

Приветствуем Вас Джона Глин с успешным полётом в космос и благополучным возвращением. Мы простая Советская семья: Я, жена, дочь Ирина и сын, который родился 20 февраля в 9 часов утра по Омскому времени; сегодня принёс жене цветы и сообщение о Вашем полёте, мы с женой решили назвать сына Джоном. Пусть наши дети растут жизнерадостными не знающими ужаса войн, пусть вместо военных аэродромов строют мирные космодромы. Пусть предстанет возможность многим людям нашей планеты увидеть её красоту с космоса.

From a Secretary in London, England

Dear Sir John!

We cannot let this notable feat of yours pass without sending you warmest congratulations and much gratitude, for inasmuch as you did it for America, you did it for us!

English people are seldom demonstrative, but always appreciative. And we certainly appreciate what you have done. We do not overlook the fact that you were backed by a great team, but in the end it was the man at the helm who carried the load.

Yours was the Day! Yours was the Glory!

From an American-Armenian in Medford, Massachusetts

The Somerville "Nejdeh" Chapter of the Armenian Youth Federation of American would like to congratulate you on being the first American to orbit the earth. To us, nothing has ever been quite as American since the signing of the Declaration of Independence. You not only made history for the United States but history for the whole world as well, and we feel that this is an inspiration, not only to Americans, but to free men everywhere. It must have been a great experience and we are glad to see that pride in our country and its accomplishments are not a thing of the past.

Well, Mr. Glenn, the Russians always wanted to be first about everything, but now the burden of the proof is on them. They thought we were failing, but you showed them, Mr. Glenn, by risking your life for God and your country.

The burden is now on the Russians. Let us see them at work, out in the open. That is another thing the Russians can learn from us, Mr. Glenn: We are not afraid of failure and do not hold it against a man. One thing is for sure, Mr. Khrushchev really got an ulcer out of all this.

We of the Somerville Chapter feel that your flight was but one step in that long process of beginning a new space era. No doubt America has an equally tough task ahead of her, that of landing safely on the moon.

Yes, Mr. Glenn, you have accomplished your mission in real true fashion but we also have a mission to accomplish, and that is to re-establish a free, independent, and united homeland for the Armenian nation. Today we are lost in the great Russian wilderness created by the Soviet but some day our prayers will also be answered and our mission fulfilled.

From a Hungarian Boy, Now Living in New York
Who Did Not Receive a Reply to His First Letter

In the happiness of your success, you should of answered my letter, however you did not done that, and with this you procured me a great delusion. Give God that to you country and to the World you do not give any delusion.

I approfit of this occasion to express my best wishes to you and to you Family for Easter.

From a Man in Sochi, U.S.S.R.

I'm very sorry that I don't have a command of English, but nevertheless I congratulate you in the way I can, from my heart; this I do on the occasion of your being America's first cosmonaut, having made a successful, remarkable, five-hour flight around the Earth!

It seems to me that your spacecraft is of special interest in that it assured the normal life activity of man, and yet the craft had a weight of only ⅓ that of our spacecraft. Also of interest is the first experience in the successful landing of a manned spacecraft on the water. I hope that the Soviet viewers will see your flight on the movie screen.

Let you and I vicariously shake hands; permit me to congratulate you once more for your victory, and wish you health and happiness.

I would be happy to receive a photo from you, and a short letter.

From an Indian Student in the U.S.S.R.

*I, a student of Peoples' Friendship University, Moscow, congrat-
ulate you on your timely, most successful flight in space. Specially
for your bravery and skill in handling the space ship.*

*We all Indian students in this university are proud of you.—ev-
ery good man should be proud of you.*

*I wish all the successes for you. I just can't explain on this paper,
my ideas & feelings, but dear Colonel—your flight was very, very
important.*

From a Man in Surrey, England

The Rainbow Bomb

I am taking the liberty of writing to you to ask, if I may, whether
you do not share with me some concern about Space bursts. As I
could hardly expect you to admit that you do, may I have the au-
dacity to appeal to you in the matter from 4 angles:—

1. *The Moral Angle.*

Many people felt very happy, I am sure, that the first "Westerner"
in Space is a good Churchman. Your own personal decision to
go into Space was, we understand from reports, not lightly taken.
Might it be possible that the success of your wonderful achievement has dimmed the recollection of the difficulty of making this
decision? Would you really have made your trip if you had known
that within a few months Americans would be exploding nuclear
devices in Space?

2. *The Scientific Angle.*

In view of the criticisms of many Scientists about these tests, is it
morally right for America, unilaterally, to take any risk in exploding Space bombs, *however slight* that risk might be thought to be.

3. *The Defence Angle.*

No doubt this borders on Security, but if there does happen to
be no direct evidence of such tests by the Russians, surely the demands of the Defence Dept. should not be acceded to.

4. *The Common Sense Angle.*

The Russians talk, perhaps sincerely, about the glories of man's future in Space. Both Americans and Russians have mentioned possible future Space co-operation. Why prejudice and endanger these great ideals before we even start? May I suggest that in these matters a responsibility may be owing to all of us who believe with you that man's only hope for the future lies in Space, also a decision not lightly reached by us.

Franked, Undated Post Card from U.S.S.R.

And this card is from me and my brother, to your brother. I want to ask just one question: "Are you poor or rich?" It is good that here everyone is equal.

From an American Living in Tokyo, Japan

When you were in orbit, I first heard that the shot was in the air when I was in Oslo, Norway. I heard more of it in Copenhagen. I then flew to Geneva but stopped in Prague. I tried to get out of the plane but was stopped by an armed guard. I pointed to the air and said, "There goes Glenn." He lowered his submachine gun and I stepped on Communist soil. At any rate, I want to express my personal appreciation for what you and the whole group have done and are doing. I have traveled the world for several years. I have heard much criticism of Americans. I never felt so proud of being an American as at that moment.

From a Japanese High-School Boy

I think that "patience" is very important and necessary when West competes with East for space contests, and discusses all kinds of problems in the world with East, and man does all sorts of things. Don't you think so?

You proved how patience is useful, great and important, which is very useful for world peoples. I think so.

It's our pride that a Japanese camera was with you in the "Friendship 7." Thank you, Mr. Glenn.

From a Newspaper Publisher in Korea

We hope that the U. S. could place a man on the moon earlier than the USSR.

President Kennedy proposed to Russia co-exploration for the moon with the U. S. and Premier Khruschev agreed to it. Do you think such co-exploration is possible? Why do you think the U. S. proposed co-exploration to the USSR?

From an Elderly Professor in Japan

Welcome to Japan! You carried out your duties of importance, directly after, in times of a public lecture in Tokyo, by television broadcast, I saw and heard longingly your gentle look and voice. I'm in ecstasy of joy. At that occasion Mrs. Glenn, son and daughter were introduced by the chairman to audience, whereupon they lively rewarded the chairman well for his services, consequently much more I increase becoming intimate with you. I'm exceedingly happy. You may be forgotten, but last year when you splendidly succeeded in space flight, immediately I wrote a congratulatory letter to you, as to this you answered to show your appreciation by cordial return of post with your fine autographed photograph and pamphlet, thus I have basked in an undeserved honor. Such terms as I am I hope to call on you and offer congratulations to you, however my body is disabled, to begin with my English is poor, in spite of I grow impatient indiscriminatley. It won't be as I wish, I'm a simple and honest aged man.

From a High-School Pupil in Indonesia

Herewith, I am as a pupil of a high school in Bandung and also in the names of many of my friends, who are your admirers.

"Wishing you a congratulation for your successful duty, as a big astronaut." We were very proud for your succeed and hope, it will be used for the science and peace among the nations.

From an Ex-Captain in the Indian Army, Living in Japan

For the past two years I've been living in a Japanese style Six-tatani room which is not much bigger than your space capsule. Last night was a unique experience following your orbital flight on a transistor receiving set the size of a cigarette pack. The program was relayed by the Armed Forces FEN (Far East Network) at Tokyo.

Your long delayed flight has certainly given the Free-world a shot-in-the-arm which it has so badly needed.

I hope you won't think too poorly of my sentiments which I've tried to express in a poetic vein.

It is only a small tribute to a wonderful guy who in turn represents an equally great country to its people.

83

The Free-world salutes you and rejoices in their pride
With His Hand upon you and our prayers beside.
The cry goes forth from hearts of all free-men
God Bless America and thy son, John Glenn!

From a Captain in the Japanese Navy

*You, in spite of several times' postponement, achieved a great
work thus far.*
*When I was reading every line of your article (and I read it again
and again very ardently) in the Japan Times, I even felt the tears
gather in my eyes.*
May our firm unity overwhelm the invasion of communists.

From a Man in Hartford, Connecticut,
Concerning Some International Matters

In the thought that you might be interested in what it says, I am
sending a clipping from the Hartford Times of yesterday which
echoes my own personal feelings about Maj. Titov, what he did—or
was reputed to have done—in the matter of space exploration.

I saw and heard you and him on television and was very little
impressed with what he had to say, particularly the manner in
which he said what he did. While you were frank and friendly as
usual it did seem to me as tho he played the part of what is known
as a "smarty pants".

Like many I have talked with I think that Russia has feet of clay
and is trying to bluff the Hell out of the rest of the world including
its accomplishments in space.

From the Australian Embassy

The Prime Minister of Australia, The Right Honourable R. G. Menzies, has asked me to convey to you on behalf of himself, his Government, and the Australian people, warm congratulations upon the magnificent success of Project Mercury. In the Prime Minister's words: "it is a triumph of great scientific and technical skill, magnificent teamwork and preparation, and outstanding human courage. Australia was happy to be able to take some part in the safety arrangements that were made."

From a Woman in Illinois

This is part of a letter written to us a few days after your flight, by a young Tokyo University freshman, our "Japanese son" by courtesy of the American Field Service International Scholarship Program. Tadatoshi Akiba lived with our family and attended our high school two years ago during his seventeenth year, and we maintain a warm relationship with him by mail. His letter contained the following words which we felt might interest you.

"Congratulations for the success of "the Friendship 7", by Commander Glen (I am not sure if the spelling or his rank is correct). I guess all the people excited beyond description. Now the human race made one more great step toward the space travel. Although your success is a little later than that of U.S.S.R., Japanese people show their highest respect to the U.S.A. for what they did in succeeding and will do. To be precise, U.S.A. has not hidden a thing, and will not in future, and treated Commander Glen as a human being, and give the important data to the scientists of the world."

I trust this is the feeling of the majority of Japanese young people rather than the rebellious attitude taken by the Student Government (the Zengakurin) whose riotous activities we read of so frequently.

From a Company in Nagasaki, Japan

We 12 members of Santo Chinaware Co. of Nagasaki experienced the disaster of the atomic bomb which resulted from the wrong use of atomic energy. We lost our parent, brothers and friends in that disaster and really wish that atomic energy will be used for no other purposes but peaceful uses.

To express our appreciation for your contribution toward the advancement of the peaceful uses of atomic energy, we decided to send you a set of coffee cups as well as to the Soviet astronauts. The design of the coffee cups was chosen by the citizens of Nagasaki by vote. We hope that you will enjoy using them.

尊敬する
グレン中佐様他二名の宇宙飛行士の皆様え

　長崎市内の陶器店に勤める私達十二名は
原子力の誤った使用をの為に原爆の悲惨さを恐しくも
身をもって体験した店員でございます
今日お贈り致しましたコーヒーセットは！

　懐い原爆で優しかった父母や兄弟それに幼い友達を
はじめふる里の長崎の町を奪の原爆で失くした被害
店員の計画で原子力の平和利用の大成果である
皆様の大偉業をたたえ　心からのお喜びをして
話し合った結果特産のコーヒーセットを被災した長崎
市民の方々からの投票で一位入選品を渡米中の
宇宙飛行士の皆様へ贈事に致しましたところ
この記事が新聞、ラジオで大々的に放送されて
市内で大反きょうを呼び好評の中に終了致しました。

　中には幼児のコンクール中の品に美しい花を
生けてくれたお姉様もいてこの
コンクールをして良かったと
全員で話し合いました
このコーヒーセットに托しました
長崎市民や私達の願いは

Imperial Palace, Tokyo

87

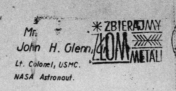

An envelope covering a letter from Omsk, U.S.S.R.
to cosmonaut John Glenn. Part of this letter is reproduced on page seventy-six.

A hand-drawn envelope design covering a letter from
an Indonesian boy. His letter is reproduced on page
sixty-five.

An envelope covering a letter from Poland, postmarked in the city of Wroclaw, and stamped "We
gather IRON scrap."

From a Young Filipino Boy

I know you are good guy and even I am only small boy I can write you. I am grade five and eleven years old and I belong in Boy Scout troop. I write I want to say I am happy to hear from voice of American you are safe and sound. My friends also very happy like me because we adopt you our Uncle Johnny before and now Uncle Johnny he make three trip around the world and return from big danger and we are glad.

For now, I be only your little mascot Johnny if you agree. I carry your things to your dressing room. I shine your boots and I go carry your message to your wife. I play with your two children if you are away and I wash dishes for Mrs. Johnny. Sometime maybe you take me up with you Johnny, I hope.

P. S. If my piggy bank has enough inside I send this by plane because a flying man like you Johnny deserve a letter with wings.

90

"ON MY HONOR,
I WILL DO MY BEST..."

CHAPTER 6

I guess there were a number of consequences of being an astronaut and taking part in the orbital flight that we did not foresee when the program started. One of the most beneficial of these has been the amount of attention that the young people and the youth groups have given to the program.

The Boy Scouts of America, in particular, have made considerable use of our endorsement of their activities to get new boys into scouting, and this seems to have had some beneficial effect. I am proud of this association, for I think the Scouts, the YMCA, the Boys Clubs of America, and some of these organizations do a wonderful job. And if one of the by-products of our space flight can be that of encouraging young people to set goals and objectives, and to take a more active part in such organizations, it is worthwhile and is an area of activity I certainly plan to encourage.

A Cub Scout from Texas Writes:

I see you all the time on television talking about scouting. I am a Cub Scout. All the boys and I wish you a speedy recovery.

I am sending you a pass to my railroad. I belong to the National Model Railroad Association. My family and I are rebuilding our layout. I wish you could see it.

From a Den Mother in Clifton, New Jersey

Last month our son became a cub scout and his mother a den mother. We were both influenced by your speeches on television concerning scouting, and I volunteered out of necessity as one parent must be active in order for the boy to be accepted.

Of all the boys in scouting in this rather large city, only ten little cub scouts represented our organization at a Veterans Day Parade held Sunday, November 10, 1963. I was the only adult connected with scouting to march. We did follow a Boy Scout band but they were from another town. When we got to the park at the end of the march, my son remarked that he wondered if Colonel John Glenn would be proud of them.

As I said before, I went into this job of necessity, but yesterday I was one of the proudest women in Clifton, because those boys marched for me.

From an Elderly Woman in California

It blessed my soul every time we saw you on TV coming out of the woods with a bunch of nice looking boy scouts and they seemed happy.

93

From The Grand Assembly,
International Order of Rainbow for Girls,
States of Washington, Idaho and Alaska

Last year our assembly presented the skit "Over the Rainbow-via Friendship Rocket." Our skit featured seven astronauts. Their names Love, Religion, Nature, Immortality, Fidelity, Patriotism and Service, representing the seven rays of the Rainbow. We also had three important officers in the control room and they were named Faith, Hope and Charity.

Our rocket was constructed by using a sit-down lawn mower covered with cardboard. On the signal "blast off" the astronaut inside started the mower and at the same time pulled the switch on a CO_2 fire extinguisher which caused smoke to come out the back. Our "Friendship 7" zoomed across the floor. The skit won us first place.

To David from a Boy Scout in Puerto Rico

I only want to know if you are now an Eagle Scout, the highest honor that a Boy Scout can have. Because I am the secretary of my Post, the other guys ask me if I could write this letter to you, but I told them it might be a difficult thing, because I wasn't sure if with the address I took from the "Scouting" magazine, the letter would reach to you, but now you can see that it has reach you.

Out boys want to know your Post Plans for this summer. We are going to make three or four camps this summer.

I think I don't have to ask your pardon for me, because I have written to you without knowing you, but my troop ask me to write you and anyway we are B.S. and I understand that we are friends.

You might be proud of a great hero as your father is. Send him a "Hello" of my part. Don't forget to answer my letter or our Post would think I am no good for a Secretary.

You can see by this letter the great trouble I have in writing english. Please pardon my way of writing and don't forget to answer the letter.

A Scoutmaster from Nebraska Writes:

As a scoutmaster, it wouldn't do for me to let Boy Scout Week go by without letting you know how much your efforts on behalf of scouting is appreciated. Your comments on the benefits of the scouting program is flashed daily by T.V. stations and it has given scouting a tremendous boost. For years we've had to combat the effects of belittling comments and jokes about Boy Scouts by unknowing adults and comedians on radio and T.V. The boys were almost ashamed to be scouts and have fun poked at them but you've made them proud to belong again and I thank you for it. The boys seem to feel that if scouting is something you and the other astronauts not only think so well of but participate in, it must be OK.

Thanks again and please continue to endorse scouting, you are making our jobs much easier.

A Mother from New Hampshire Writes:

What we do want to say to you is this—that you did more for scouting in a few minutes on television than you can possibly imagine. Scouting, so we are told, is being belittled all over the country and in our town in New Hampshire, boys who continue in it are called "sissies" by some high school students.

A Woman from Louisiana Writes:

Your public appearances as an astronaut and then as a Boy Scout officer have endeared you to Americans who appreciate genuine Christian character and patriotism. I wish for the youth of our nation thousands more such men as examples, to challenge them to live decent purposeful lives. It seems to me that the 65 million drinking Americans are having too much impact on our youth.

I believe, furthermore, that it is utterly foolish for the President and his Council on Physical Fitness to ignore the weakening effects of ethyl alcohol as a beverage. Mr. Glenn, how can any man or group of men seriously talk of wanting our youth to be physically fit if they remain silent about the dreadful effects of beverage alcohol? If a youth does grow up with physical fitness as a goal, how is he to know that his drinking of alcohol will tear down all he has tried to build up in the way of good health? A CURTAIN of silence has been drawn about the true scientific effects of ethyl alcohol as a beverage.

FEARS,
WANTS—
AND
HOPE

CHAPTER 7

The "Hope" of the title to this chapter comes not only from the hope sought in some of the letters you'll read here; but also from this letter *to Annie* from one of the greatest comedians of all time—Bob Hope.

From Bob Hope

It was quite a thrill, to talk to you and to your MAN-OF-THE-DAY, the other night.

I want you to see the monologue I did on our last show as I thought you'd get a kick out of it. I know John doesn't need any jokes. I've heard him and he's well stacked. . . . . . in every way.

Again, our heartiest congratulations and thanks.

Thank you, thank you very much . . . how do you do, ladies and gentlemen. . . . You know, I'll be satisfied if this is the *second* greatest television show this month.

Yessir, Colonel John Glenn made it . . . now let's see if we can launch this one, huh.

But wasn't it wonderful? That space shot? I don't know about you . . . but for the first time I'm happy about paying taxes . . . I really am.

No, but I thought it was just great. Incidentally, Colonel Glenn feels great . . . but he's developed a terrific craving for bananas.

The flight made history. Imagine an American going around the world without a checkbook?

Every television set in the nation was turned on. When there is something worthwhile to watch, people are interested. That's not a joke, that's a note I got from my sponsor.

But you've got to hand it to Glenn. He's the bravest Marine since John Wayne.

No, it was a great space achievement . . . and it was also quite an advance in medical history. We found out what happens when a capsule takes a man. (Applause)

No, but what an event . . . can you imagine . . . seventeen thousand five hundred miles an hour . . . and he's not even a teen-ager.

No, he circled the earth three times. He had to . . . there were no off ramps.

And he was three and a half hours getting off the ground. He left the ignition key in his other pants.

But the trip was very smooth. Of course he left early in the morning when there was no traffic.

And he flew over Las Vegas three times. It was the only place nobody looked up.

Not only that, he passed Japan three times without buying a camera.

He got a little hammy at one point. Going over New Concord, Ohio, he said, "Look Ma . . . no hands."

I thought it was wonderful . . . did you read where he was kidding with his fellow astronauts? Imagine, 160 miles out in space and he calls headquarters for flight pay. He's worse than Jack Benny during a station break.

No, can you imagine him in that tiny capsule telling jokes? Who holds his idiot cards?

That's all I need . . . a supersonic Soupy Sales.

And he got $245 for five hours' traveling . . . that Jimmy Hoffa moves everywhere, I wanna tell you.

How about that food they gave him . . . a tube of meat paste and a tube of fruit paste. We spend eighty million dollars for the missile and then send the pilot tourist.

No, he had a bottle of malted milk pills. That's what they claimed they were . . . he was awfully high.

He must have been pretty high. When he got back they found a harp string caught on one of the curb feelers.

I just wanna say, along with the rest of the world, I, personally want to congratulate Colonel John Glenn. And it's comforting to know that when he gets back to Arlington, Virginia, his wife will still tell him how to drive.

An Elderly Woman from Trevose, Pennsylvania, Writes:

Let me share a quotation I found, a few days ago, in James Thurber's writings: "It takes guts to be happy."

To President John F. Kennedy
from a Company President in Austin, Texas

Instead of giving Lt. Col. Glenn a bunch of words and a medal why don't you give the man a set of Eagles and take the Oak Leaves off.

He and his kids and lovely wife can be proud of that, and they can eat with it, when the medals and praise are hard to trade at a grocery store.

100

From a Californian
Who Read a Cigarette Advertisement and
Mistook Glenn for One of the Men in the Picture

I was so glad to get your letter today telling me that you are not the Mr. Glenn in the picture of Apr. 21 in Look Mag.

It does look a lot like you and I think that is why the Cigarette Co used it and put no name under it.

My comment:

I had several letters on this one "taking me apart" for supposedly letting my picture be used in cigarette advertising.

On checking the advertisement referred to, the subject in the picture did look somewhat like me (he did have more hair, I'm sorry to say) but the silver suit and helmet he held were those of a deep-sea diver. I don't know whether there was intended deception by the cigarette and advertising companies, but they necessitated my sending several replies to irate citizens assuring them I was not, as one man put it, "on the weed," and had not "sold my soul for cigarette gold."

A Blind Seventh-Grade Student from Chicago Writes:

As you said at the parade in New York, on March 1, you and the other astronauts are representing all Americans as you make your spectacular flights. That's why I would like to personally congratulate and thank you for a great job, well done.

I have enclosed with this letter a paper with the brail alphabet and one with each of your family's names on it. Any symbol not appearing in the alphabet is a capital, a period or a braille contraction.

101

A Very Young Girl from
Dolton, Illinois, Writes via Her Mother

. . . *Yesterday morning when you sailed up into space, I must confess I wasn't particularly impressed. You see I'm only fifteen months old and frankly a girl my age has many other things to think about besides space craft.*

However I guess you must be somebody special because my mommy and daddy got up at 5:30 in the morning for you and they weren't even crabby and believe me, when I used to get them up at that hour they were far from cheerful (even though I was close to starvation!)

I know you are real busy but maybe someday you'll have a chance to drop a line or two, and maybe by then I'll be able to read a little better.

A Mother from North Carolina Writes:

One thing's got me puzzled. If astronaut pertains to a male what would a girl be called should their be one and I'm sure some gal will eventually be the first.—I was wondering would we perhaps call her —"lasstronaut"?

From an Ex-Marine in Cape Canaveral

While working for the Electrical concern at Cape Canaveral, wiring the complexes in 1957 and 1958, my Fiancee and I had a beautiful Diamond ring made in the form of an atlas missile, and there had been no indication at that time there would be 7 Astronauts, but this ring was made with 7 diamonds. It is a beautiful "Dinner Ring", and the stones are perfect Blue-white stones. As far as I know, this is an exclusive, it being our own design.

From a Man in Providence, Rhode Island

I have had a rather interesting experience which involves you, and which I thought might be interesting to you.

I was in the Canadian Wilderness during the latter part of May on a fishing trip. We were completely out of touch with civilization, and could not usually even get audible radio reception, so we were unaware of Scott Carpenter's three-orbit trip until several days after the event, when we picked up a very faint news broadcast.

My guide, an Indian Named Joe, spoke very little English, and understood only an occasional word in our native tongue. He could not read or write, in any language, and he communicated in a mixture of French and a local Indian dialect.

The day that we heard of Carpenter's success I wanted to share the news with Joe, but I was far from convinced that he had ever heard of such things as orbital flights, for he came from a remote Indian Village in Northern Quebec. I decided to have a try at it anyway, and while we were quietly paddling across a wilderness pond I said, "Joe. You know about astronauts?"

A Blank, stupid expression spread over his face, and he said "No".

I said, "You know of cosmonauts?"

"Non." Another Blank.

"Man go around world?" With hand gestures by me.

"non."

Breaking into my finest French, which leaves much to be desired linguistically, I said, with gestures, "Joe. L'Homme go round Le Mond in capsool. You understand?"

I was still not getting through to him, as his stupid facial expression vividly testified.

After throwing several more words at the poor Indian, each of which are in everyday use in our papers, and each of which had a connection with space flight, I found I had made no progress whatever in getting my "news flash" through to Joe.

Suddenly an inspiration came to me. "Joe. You ever hear of John Glenn?"

The effect on Joe was like the sun coming through on a cloudy day. His bronzed face lit up with a very satisfied grin of comprehension, and he said, "Ah. Oui. Jean Glenn. Je comprend. Bon Homme. Bon Homme!"

Joe was finally in the ball game, so I pressed on with my incomprehensible French. "Joe. Cette Jeudi un autre Homme go round Le mond Meme as John Glenn. Scott Carpenter."

"Ah. Oui? Charpentier? C'est Bonne, c'est Bonne."

I had finally made it, and Joe, I am sure, was as excited about the news as I was.

Nothing could be more remote from the quiet solitude of the Canadian Wilderness than the excitement and tension of orbital flight, yet this kindly, uneducated Indian, in his own retarded way, considered the name John Glenn just as much of a household word as do the rest of us who call ourselves civilized, though he had apparently never heard of any of the other common words or phrases having to do with the space program.

I thought this little incident might interest you, as it did me. When you make your next orbital trip, and if you pass over the wilds of Quebec, wave a little hand at Joe, for he, like all the rest of the world's peoples, will be with you all the way.

To President John F. Kennedy from a Missourian

Honor the hero with the two great tunes—The National Anthem and:—"He's got the whole world in his hands."

From a Woman in Ohio

May the parents of America and the world profit by this noble example set by John and Annie Glenn.

Just an added note—I thot it might interest you to know that the children here at the State Blind School where I work, sat quietly as the count down was nearing 0. In home economics class they were given molding clay to work with as they listened and what do you suppose 2 of them molded. One made a spaceship and one a woman kneeling in prayer with her hands folded and face turned uptoward the heavens. Some with partial vision watched TV.

A Housewife and a Witness
from Brisbane, Australia, Write:

We are surprised to find that very few people apparently witnessed your historic flight in space, so far as your journey across the Australian continent is concerned, and as my husband and I both were fortunate enough to do so, feel that you and your wonderful family may be interested in knowing about it.

It was a humbling experience to know that in that bright "star" away in outer space, a very brave man was orbiting the earth, facing so many dangers in the cause of science, humanity, and may we hope, Peace. I wish we could have flashed this message to you then and there, as we whole-heartedly say it now—"John Glenn, we salute you."

From a Girl in California

Thank you—
Sincerely & how!
                wow!
P.S.: Please forgive, you leave me speechless!

From a Psychiatrist in Los Angeles

Perhaps you would be interested in a psychiatric suggestion regarding space travel.

I believe there must be felt a need for greater physical comfort during the exposure to the isolation and emptiness of space. You would be the best one to have judgment in this respect. If so, then I would advise to make certain that the uniforms, seats, and food should be quite similar to those of an infant, and the seemingly stiff and compressing space suits should be replaced.

I am enclosing a publication on "Kinesthetic Needs in Infancy."

105

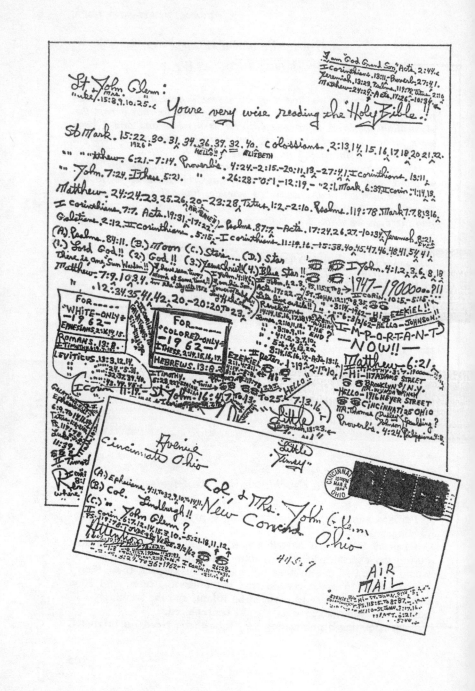

To "GUTS" GLENN

U.S.A.

FROM THE ORDINARY
BLOKE IN THE STREET

AN OPEN LETTER.

SINCERE, BUT PATHETIC

One of our greatest health problems as a nation is that of mental health, so let me state at the outset that I have no intent of making light of people who are obviously mentally unbalanced. But they do send mail, and this can be a shock to the recipient. The only purpose in including this section is that it does reflect a type of mail we received and, as such, was extremely interesting to us, even though much of it is very pathetic. The earnestness and sincerity expressed are impressive. And they are trying their best to communicate some of their deeply felt emotions and thoughts to us.

I have been told by a psychiatrist that one of the methods used these days to help the mentally disturbed work out their problems and to get them rehabilitated for possible return to normal living, is to have current events discussions. This helps them to readapt for a return to the world of reality. The orbital flight of Friendship 7 was obviously one event that was discussed by some of these people. We received many letters from those obviously burdened with mental problems beyond their control. One disturbing note with regard to this mail was that most of it did not come from institutions, but apparently was sent by people living in open society.

There is obviously little we could do for the people, much as we regretted it. I include these letters only to let you share with us some of the shock, regret, elation, and sympathy we felt for these people as we opened the mail. There was another category that we received along this same line that has not been included in the book. That included pornographic mail or that which made various suggestions to members of the family that are not printable for general reading.

A Faith Healer from Seattle, Washington, Writes:

. . . let me tell you of an experience I had over 20 yrs. ago, I left my body one night and went out in space as you did but without the Space Ship. A voice said to me that I was 780 miles out there looking back at our beautiful earth revolving on its axis.

Anonymous from Welland, Ontario

I wrote Werner Von Braun about seeing a Russian? Rocket landing on the moon. I would like to tell some further important details. I saw it going around the moon and then I saw it pause and where it paused I saw a small speck of light appear. Did they launch a tiny satellite of the moon? Could this satillite repel and send away from the moon any rocket trying to land on it. Because on its next round of the moon when it went to go up toward the tiny spark its nose was diverted out into space. It paused and working controls? straightened went up to the spark, paused, to check it? went on around the moon and landed on the lower left hand corner of the moon releasing 3 red lights, one floated into space but sputtered, went out. Enclosed is a picture of it.

Anonymous from San Diego

I'se jest got to tell you what dem flakes you saw are. I's born with the veil over my face and I can tell you things you smart people down in that cape don't know and never will know.

Last night I got a dream right from heaven—bout dem specks. De are the children you never learn the lesons here de should have got, so when de get to that golden gate Peter knows de are not ready and he tel then der punismet is to go in orbitt and spin around until de gets their lesson befo de can get to heven.

Der all so much he had to make then just small speks—is what de is —that is what you see.

When you try to got to the moon aint no busnes you what is there any way—God make that to give us light by day and no busnes of yours how he makes hit shine—but I suspicon you will never get thro the many spcks to will find in the far out up there. So many people have been worce that God wants us to be.

So pleas tel the smart elects down at that cape to spend more mony and the poor on this world and stop putin ther nose in gods heaven.

Our God is in heven—and he does what pleases him, Sams bible, so you best try and pleas him and stop mesing up his beuty.

From a Man in New York

Until now I have been unable to present my ideas to the right peo-ple. My ideas or theories have been considered as being unconven-tional or deviate from accepted theories and even of being too early. Now I believe I have found the man who may see it the way I do. Because to you, unconventionality and controversy carry little weight, and the things you do are those ahead of our time.

I have a variety of theories. However, what I refer to above is in the field of flight and aviation. It is a theory about the nature or behavior of air. Controversial as it seems, it will solve all the phe-nomena of air, such as the hypersonic heat of re-entry, 'sonic boom' of high speed aircraft and even the fire ball and ice crystal shroud of atomic bomb.

The development of intense heat during re-entry, whether it is due to friction *as generally believed or due to* compression *as my theory points out, seems irrelevant for operation. However, if a theory can tell how the heat is actually developed and will lead the way to a 'Cool Re-entry' instead of a 'Fire Ball' re-entry, as you described it, it should be worthy of investigation.*

As we all know that a low orbiting missile is slowed down gradu-ally by skimming the thin air repeatedly at each of its perigee. And

110

is burned off only when it is plunging into the atmosphere. Innocent as this happening may seem, it has pointed out to us that the skimming of thin air with even orbiting speed will not produce burning temperature. Therefore, if we can maintain skimming to slow down the vehicle but avoid plunging, we can also avoid burning.

No one is willing to travel into space, knowing that when he comes back the civilization of the mother earth will not be there any more! Yes, this may happen if we are not farsighted enough to identify an approaching catastrophe so great that it can wipe out our civilization.

The common enemy I discover is so enormous that no single country or combination of countries will be able to fight it. It requires a whole world to withstand it. This common enemy is always there and it has caused the destruction of this world several times in the past and is threatening us now. It is the world's worst enemy—The Ice Age! Our trouble now is our unability to foresee how it will behave, how destructive it will be, and when it will happen.

Realizing the awesomeness of the ice age, I often wish that my theory should prove to be wrong. Nevertheless, we have to be certain about it. In fact the exploration of the ice age will benefit not just a few individuals or a group of people, but the whole human race. Most important still is the saving of our civilization which all of us have had share in making and some are most proud of their share like yourself. This civilization takes more than 5,000 years in its development, I wish that it will not be lost just by mere ignorance or distrust among peoples.

A Woman in Ohio Writes:

Love is Gravity—it holds things together. Can man make gravity in space capsule.

I believe so strongly that God's love is gravity that if I were to be shot in space God would fill my space ship with gravity and I would be held by him in my seat and would not be weightless.

111

From a Woman in St. Petersburg, Florida

I am commanded by the Queen to thank you very much for the First Day cover with Colonel Glenn's autograph which you have sent for The Prince of Wales.

A Post Card from a Man in New York

CASH NEEDED

My dear Sir:

May God grant that we meet in heaven. People like you and your two pals destined to be guinea pigs are 100 demon possessed. It is almost impossible for them to go to heaven, because like Nixon they would have to have some people interested enough in their soul's salvation to dunk them 100 times to scare them into doing it themselves in holy horror of sin, crying "God be merciful to me the sinner," obeying thus Acts 2:38 q.v.

Male Armchair Traveler from Arizona

Dear Sir:

Lets take a little trip OK?
ZONG—here we are in space about equidistant from several stars of which our sun is one
How you like it out here Colonel?
No shade trees
No night   Just high noon, now forever and no let up
?What Sir? "no place for man or beast"
Pardon Sir? "Why did I want to come out here"?
Sir I thought we might find some stardust in this area.

From a Canadian to President Kennedy:

Dear Mr. United States:
This unique spacial adverture has delighted my heart, soul, spirit and mind; as I know it must have delighted hundreds of millions of millions more, from both a personle and scientific standpoint.

This flight I consider as the most significant of all orbital flights; and the basis of my reasoning is this, this consideration also takes into its logic any failyour that may have been encountered, which thank God has not been the case in this scientific mile stone.

First of all it was most significant, because the impulse of the event was being recorded by the conscious pulsating rythm in the heart of the peoples; mental experiance; thus it has been enhanced by this telopathic information;

In conclusion,

IT BEARS THE UNIVERSAL NATURE OF A WORLD WIDE COSMIC IMPORTANCE.

Congratulations JOHN GLENN
From the pen of the Divine Psychology and Philosophy OF THIS ENLIGHTENED AGE.

Female Love-Power Believer from Wellton, Arizona

This letter may appear to be a bit of a crack-pot one, but after riding with you on your glorious trip thru space and meeting all your wonderful family, I feel that you will look into the matter a little deeper. I know that it is your great desire and that of ALL of us to get to the Moon, for various reasons one of them being to beat the Russians. Hence anything that can be done to help that should be followed up. I have on very good authority, a way that will fascilitate our program and achieve it within a period of two years.

I have the humble honor and privilege of being a "automatic writer" or "amanuensis". (Which I am told can be done by anyone if they go about it properly) and was told that "there is not enough love power" being engenerated by us. If we could turn our enphasis on using the trip to the moon to help humanity and not only to beat the Russians and use space militarily, our successes would be greater and the necessary information and formulas would be coming. I feel a particular urge to approach you or someone among you who could justifiably bring up the subject in connection with our next scheduled imminent departure for outer space. Would you like to try an experiment amongst all you highly trained men, to specifically LOVE all your parts in your craft, the ticklish ones, the personnel who send you, and mankind as you try to set a record time in the outer zones. I am specifically directed to tell you to ask "all the technitians to send out thots of LOVE to the Russians as the capsul goes thru the last three turns and it will be a great success" Have no fear. Our man will not be lost and will return alive.

With scientific research now being done on the effect Love has on even plants growth, I feel you will not scorn this as an idle suggestion. I am sure your Mother will have much to add to this. In the meantime please reassure the family of our next adventurer in outer space and tell them, with their help he will have a great fund of knowledge to add to our increasing store.

From New York City

The Christ Spirit of the dog, RIN TIN TIN, who announced himself as spokesman for the dog that perished in a space capsule last week.

I come this day to represent the animal kingdom of the animals that have God intelligences, that have passed from the physical world of the Earth to the Spirit domain of everlasting life. The Fatherhead of the Tree of Life has given every creature in the animal kingdom the same God evolvement as the human beings made in His image and likeness, known as men. I, Rin Tin Tin, send forth my Light to all the animals that are on your Earth today.

I come this day to announce to you that the High Selves of these animals could be of primary importance, in that they would come through and answer many important questions that only these animals would know the answer to. For instance, the dog that was sent into outer space last week would have reported to the personnel that were in charge of that particular phase of the space operation, that the central heating system was too hot for the animals to survive in the capsule. The wirings of the filaments were built too close to the surface of the walls. The intense heat of the space capsule got too hot after it was in flight for a certain length of time in space. The heat regulating system was not perfected, as it was supposed to be. There was a choice of heating systems; this particular one that was used in that flight will never be perfected. The engineers must perfect a heating system that will not accelerate itself after it has reached a higher level of altitude in the sky. There must be a better type of coating of protection in the wires themselves.

I would suggest that the scientists use the dogs known as FOX TERRIERS. They have, for some reason which I won't go into here, a better resistance to heat. Certain dogs are better adjusted to heat than others.

RIN TIN TIN
Yours in the Light of
The Eternal Father GOD

A Man from Richmond, Virginia, Writes:

This is a very important letter to our nation if you will notice the contents of this letter closely, and do as I request, and in the process of time you will find that you'll have an easy way to come back out of space with out any danger—

Here is what I have to say I have Russias complete rocket system, including the power that they use and the way it is used. I also have the blue prints of their rockets and space craft. Also their system of coming back from space with out a parechut.

Colonel Glenn, I want to get this in our governments pocession as soon as possible and before you mention this to any one I want to come to your house in Arlington and show you that I do have what I say and can produce the same at request of the Government. I don't want to be known to no one but your family. I do not want it to be known that I have entered your house until a time that I would be safe. I guarentee that I can produce what I have said that I could.

115

I am coming to Washington and I am hoping to call you on the phone and arrange to see you at your house without being seen. I will call you and use the name Mr. . . . when I call.

This is all true Col. Glenn, and I can quickly prove it to you on arrival at your home. Then you can help me see the President the *only man* that I will deal with. I will pay you well for doing it.

From a Man in Portland, Oregon

The proper planet to aim at is planet Pluto. That is the planet Our God and Creator Genesus 1: 1-Holy Bible wants us to land a rocket on. There is a definite reason for doing so.

Pluto is the planet that has been made ready for the inhabitance of man, and there must be "Seed" planted there.

A Man from Baltimore Writes:

A few days ago, I was told of an incident occurring at the time of John's orbiting the earth which, I think, may interest you. This was related by an acquaintance who is employed at a local mental institution.

One phase of the therapy practiced at this hospital is the reading of news items to the patients followed by a round-table discussion, pro and con, the news of the day. This is done, so I've been told, to minimize the feeling of isolation that often plagues these unfortunate people.

After the exciting details of the flight of the Friendship VII was read to the group, there was a most unusual silence. All sat and stared fixedly at the therapist for several minutes. Finally, one asked, "Now, why would any man pull a fool stunt like that one?" Before the therapist could answer, another spoke up, "I don't know, but we can ask him when they bring him in!"

And so sure were the patients that John would eventually arrive that one bunking next to the only empty bed in the ward went to the superintendent and asked to be moved. Said he didn't want to be next to "that nutty star-gazer."

the END oF the WorlD will
Come June 12, 1964

Hello John Glenn
Yes; you John Glenn probley
dont quite Remember, and that is
of the warning Message of which
I sent to you Befor you went
up to orbit around The World,
yes you can now see of what
happened to you Because of
neglecting my message, John not
only you I sent the message to
But all of the other Astronauts
I have warned many of others
of DiFFerent things But No one
Listens to what I tell Them or
of the messages I send or
Give to them

Signed the
Son of God

Comments Re: Flight of John Glenn
to the President; from a Man in Hemet, California

Watching the show put on at our expense of sending John Glenn
into orbid. How stupid you expect us to be to believe that he is going around in orbid and he recovered. My opinion is that it is nothing but a fake take off. Oh he may have gone a couple miles.? or
was dropped from low level into the ocean and then make believe
he is recovered! from orbid around the earth. boloney! Watching the
capsul traveling through the air makes it radicalous! So why don't
you stop wasting our money on something impossible! Spend it on
research on medicine and real things like planes, Atom Bombs
and other defense that we believe in! Also wasting money going to
the moon. No one will ever make that either! It is not to be and
never will be!

"WHEN YOU MARRIED ME . . ."

"When you married me . . ." To open a letter and find that someone thinks I am her husband, even though we have never met, is a little disconcerting to say the least. And this has happened with a number of letters. The psychiatrists explain this as a not too unusual phenomenon of mental illness. A person who has lost a husband or a wife will sometimes crack under the strain and transfer those thoughts or affections to another person. This, however, does not make it any less disconcerting when you happen to be the object to whom they transfer this affection. It is a pathetic thing and there was little I could do, but it is one type of mail that we received.

Other things have occurred in the romantic letter line where people have expressed their love and affection in no uncertain terms, not just to me but to other members of my family. And there have been a few examples of that included here. One of the difficulties provoked by such people is that you never know what may happen in public. On one occasion I had to take special precautions. A woman had written as though she were my wife, incorporating very intimate details of our "life together," had sent several letters, and had called NASA concerning her planned visit to me. Security was alerted, of course, even though she lived several hundred miles away. But then I was scheduled to give an address and lead a discussion only about fifteen miles from her hometown. This posed some problems because I had visions of her trying to join me on the platform as my wife, with "our" daughter, etc., and making some other move that might be highly embarrassing. In that particular case, to protect all parties concerned, she was kept under surveillance until I was in and out of the area. And

119

as far as I know she never even knew that she was being watched. This same person has wanted to visit me a number of times and has set times and airline schedules for her arrival but fortunately has never arrived.

Another tack for this romantic interest is that several men have written to express their extremely amorous intentions toward my daughter, Lyn.

The examples above concern persons with obvious difficulties, but another occurrence shows that what starts as an apparent mental problem is not always so, and it indicates the extent to which some perfectly normal people will go. I received a letter from a girl who described in great detail the events surrounding a visit she and I supposedly had on "Morning Star Beach." This description included how we watched the sun come up together after a night on "Morning Star Beach," and what she thought of the whole visit. She enclosed her picture and was a very nice looking young lady, *indeed*. But I have never been to Morning Star Beach, and my first thought was that she had some delusions. Reading on, however, it became apparent that someone had been misrepresenting himself as me. On the advice of several officials I turned the matter over to the postal authorities. They, in turn, investigated and after tracking down letters, people, and places, found that there was an officer in one of the armed services who had been on leave at the time and had been visiting Morning Star Beach. He looked a little like me, and passed himself off as being John Glenn, secretly on leave at Morning Star Beach for a rest. From events as described in her letter he was having quite an eventful leave, and not much rest, until the postal authorities made contact with him. There is reason to believe he will not so misrepresent himself again, they tell me. At least not with my name.

From a Woman in Indiana

When you married me, you took over half of my job, that of teaching mentally retarded children, deaf children, and newly weds. This is done by a transmitter that has been placed in my head. My thoughts, what my eyes see, and what I hear can be seen on television. So you see, darling I don't just want you I need you for I can't do this alone. I must admit as of right now the job isn't paying very much, but I am trying to do something about that and getting no where it seems.

SECOND LETTER:

I know I was confused for awhile, and I know we must be able to face realities. My trouble seemed to be I had reality confused with memory. Because I could not remember marrying you I pretended to believe I wasn't and yet I felt as married as anyone could possabal be.

THIRD LETTER:

I have imagined at least a hundred times what it will be like the first time I meet you as John, and I don't suppose any of them are near what it will really be like. The way I like least of all is where you say "I'm sorry I don't know you. I have a wife Annie, and we have been married nineteen years." I will look at you and I will know you are lying. You will look at me and you will know that I know you are lying, but I won't be able to prove it. The way I like best is where you say "Honey, what took you so long?"

To Lyn from a Lonely Boy in Maryland

Lynn, My Lynn,
I love you so as you will know how I feel towards you.

121

From a Woman in Massachusetts

I sent a picture like this to a near-by Air Force base in hopes of finding two stray Air Force men who might enjoy the company of two such charming women as my sister and myself, but evidently everyone is happily dated there. It really is tough being "thirtyish" without the companionship of eligible males. You being such a hero of mine (at my age too!!), I wanted you to have this in case there are any stray Marines around the Boston area.

From a Young Girl in Maryland

I saw you when you went up into space. I think you are very, very handsome. I always said the one that marries you is very lucky. I guess Annie is the one that got you. I really do think you are very, very, very, handsome. I am 10 and I am in 5th grade. I wrote a book about you. Will you please write a letter back to me. I will be very happy.

From a Family in Chestertown, New York

Hearty congratulations to you and the space project crew from ____ Chestertown, N.Y. (County of Warren)!!!

Chestertown is a very small town! Five hundred in all—taking in surrounding lake and resort areas.

Everyone hopes that all future attempts to explore space will be as successful!!!

As for myself, I wish I were Mrs. Glenn (your wife) so that I could congratulate you with a great big kiss!! However, my family and I will probably never be fortunate enough to even shake your hand!

You have made everyone in the United States proud to be "Yankees!

Our Very very best to the entire family (your mom and dad, your wife's parents, your daughter Lyn, son David, and of course your wonderful wife!!! They are truly the top crew!! God bless you all!!!

P.S. Colonel Glenn, My father is quite a "bug" about space. It is his favorite hobby or passtime when he is not busy as electrical contractor (the best in Chestertown)! Dad can hardly wait til spring and summer and fall come so he can get his telescope out!! He has a wonderful time and soon has a crowd of neighborhood folks gathered around!

GIFTS AND CRAZY ADDRESSES

I wish we had started keeping a log of all the unusual and crazy addresses, for we don't have too many of the good examples here. I was surprised at some of the ingenious methods people use for putting addresses on envelopes, and I am certain the mailmen who have to decipher some of these things must hate us with a passion. But an event such as this seems to challenge the ingenuity in people to see what unusual addresses they can use. One letter we received just had a picture clipped from a newspaper and placed on the envelope as the address. Another one, mailed in Europe, was mailed to Glenn USA. Some people have clipped different colored letters from ads and magazines and have formed the address by that means.

But along with this, one of the most interesting things has been the transition in formality or, I should say, lack of formality as time has gone by since the flight. This has been noticeable, not only in the mail, but also in being in public in crowds, or with children, or with different groups we have visited. At the time of the flight, the usual salutation we would read or would hear seemed to be, "Lieutenant Colonel John Glenn." But as time went on, it seemed many people started feeling as though they knew us even better, and the salutation would be just to "John Glenn," and now if we're out in a crowd we most often hear, "Hi John," or "Hi Annie." The letter addresses have reflected the lessening of formality. And that suits us fine.

There has been considerable confusion in some people's minds as to which astronauts were on what flights. And I have received mail addressed to SXX Shepard Glenn, Carpenter Glenn, Grissom Glenn or Dear Lt. Col. John Allen, to Dear Admiral Glenn, Lt. Glenn, 1st Lt. Glenn, Dear

Uncle Glenn, Dear and Most Famous Lt. Col. Glenn, and one from France to *Astronaute Extraordinaire*. Some use terms associated with the space program, such as Dear Mr. Space Man or the Orbit Man.

We received many gifts, and one of the most unusual came in a big black notebook. This notebook was filled with over 175 envelopes postmarked from different towns in the United States. These were collected and assembled by a woman in Texas, and placed in the proper sequence to tell the story of the orbital flight. The reproductions of postmarks on the end papers of this book, then, are more than a pretty design. They represent some of the postmark story, when the names of the towns are read in sequence. I am sure you will agree with me that this required a lot of work and was a most ingenious means of relating the events of 20 February '62. Here is the way the whole postmark story of the flight reads:

GLENN-RIDDLE

Glenn Wake Early, Shook Sleepy-Eye. Felt Fine. Haddam Bath. Eaton Orange, Toast, Anmoore. Hima Hungry-Horse. Dresden Silver Overall. Combs Flat-Top Bald-Knob. Glendon Helmet. Haddock Williams Douglas Check Glen-Head; Heartwell, Armstrong, Livermore Normal. Van Driver Hurry Cross-City. Weathers All-good, Cloudy Skyline Goodway Due-West. Atlas Ready. Glenarm Waves, Mount-Calm, Glen-Springs Ina Friendship. Counts Downs Start. (Tenstrike, Nine-Points, Eight-mile, Seven-Mile, Six-Mile, Five-Points, Four-Mile, Three-Notch, Two-Dot). Cut-And-Shoot. Glen-Rose Point-Blank, Defiance Gravity Laws. Glen-Elder Pray, Mummie Echo, Anna Manifest Faith, Young-America Wishon Star. Glenview Continental-Divide, Poland-Mines, French-Broad, German-Valley, English Center, Stillmore, Speedwell Onaway. Neversink Hells-Half-Acre. Half-way, Lone-Wolf Spot Evening-Shade Andarko Black-Earth Show-Low. Perth Offerman Light. Electric-City Burnt-Hills, Burnt-Woods, Burnt-Cabins Light-Street. Bloomingburg Signal Ship-Bottom. Glen-Echo Harrah, What-Cheer. Cape-Canaveral Askew Argo? Okay, Igo Onemo Tripp Round-O Globe (Glenhope). Lookout Window-Rock(et) White Spot Goby. (Learned Painton Alloy Peel). Mango Circle Earth. Three-Point Triumph Glendo Shock Moscow, Red-Devil Turney Green. Mission Success. Glendive, Glen-Rock, Glenburn, Glen-Cross, Glenwhite. Pilot Aimwell Randolph Center Atlantic. Put-In-Bay. Seaman Rescue Blooming-Glen. Happy-Jack Kennedy Telephone The-Glen. "Great Works, Job Weldon." Traveller-Rest.

From a Woman in Missouri

I have a pedigreed black male cocker spaniel who is 3-½ years old and I cannot keep him anymore. I would be glad to give him to you.

From a Young Boy in Long Island, New York

Would you like to have one of our first born kittens in the space capsule? Am wondering if you and the rest of the Astronauts would like to have an Astrocat each.

From a Mother in Dallas, Texas

This little medal has been blessed and has been my lucky piece for years and years. Please accept it so the blessing and luck that I've had heretofore will be yours forever.

From a Young Girl in Sanford, North Carolina

I heard over T.V. that the U.S. didn't give you a purple heart since you fell in the bathroom. I have made a purple heart because I think you deserve one. I didn't know which kind of heart so I made two.

From a Company in St. Petersburg, Florida

We are enclosing one of our new conditioning suits, that can be a help to you in your training. It is also a windbreaker to keep you from drying out while working out in cold windy weather.

127

From a Young Lady in Ridgefield, Connecticut

Recently I was visiting in Virginia and I was hoping I could meet you but unfornately you were not home. By the way—I hope you received the azelia plant.

From a Company in Hollis, Queens, New York

We were so proud and moved by your successful orbital flight in February, 1962 and, in appreciation of the kindness shown by the people of Perth, Western Australia, who lighted the way for you, we made an offer of a gift our silicone rubber implant grade materials used in Retinal Detachment surgery to the hospitals in this fair city which perform eye surgery.

From a Trading Corporation in Taipei, Taiwan (Formosa)

To express our admiration, we have taken the liberty to weave, specially for the occasion, a Ramie Rug, 3′ × 5′, depicting the space ship in flight. This rug contains about 75,000 knots, each knot being tied by hand, and the design was formed by employing different colored yarns.

From a Woman in Sharon, Pennsylvania

It would give me great pleasure to introduce and present to you the first little Astronaut, a (Trilobite) 450 million years old. The first living thing on this Earth which you have so successfully encircled.

Arnhem 11 februari 1962

To Mr Major Astronaut John Herschel Glenn
Cape Caneverel U.S.A.

Dear Major Glenn

This evening I saw you at the
television you and your family
I am a dutch boy of fifteen
years old and I collect all the news of
space-flights and rackets
Please can you send me a
photo with your signature which I saw
at the television
When you like it, I will send
you a pair of Dutch wooden shoes.
I wish you a very good flight
and good luck!
Kind regards to you and your
family.

Bart Vos   Bart Vos.
Joris van de Haagenlaan 42.
Arnhem.
Holland..

From Limaville, Ohio

This is to certify:

LT. COL. JOHN H. GLENN, JR. HAS BEEN GRANTED ONE HUNDRED
ACRES OF LAND ON THE MOON

Property is located on the edge of beautiful Atomic Crater and
will be available as soon as radioactive fallout settles.
Grantee has been chosen because of his active interest in: moon-
shining; howling at the moon; love of green cheese; desire to get
the hell away from it all and ability to get higher than a kite.

PROPERTY DEED SHALL BE VOIDED IF NOT HOMESTEADED 24 HOURS
UPON RECEIPT

ALL HOUSE UNDER SUPERVISION OF FHA (FARAWAY HOUSING AD-
MINISTRATION) issued *20th* day of *February, 1963.*

From an Artist in Vancouver, Washington

My paintings are not for sale. However, I do give them away
where they will be most appreciated.
Right now I am considering doing your portrait responding to the
cheers of your class of 39 in the gym at New Concord Muskingum
College. With the idea of course to present it to them as a gift. Will
you please tell me, what are your school colors there?

"I HAVE THIS PROBLEM..."

CHAPTER 8

Sharing troubles and difficulties with another person must indeed be one of the sincerest forms of flattery. It shows that the person writing the letter trusts and confides in someone he thinks may in some way be able to help. In some of the letters people told us of problems and troubles that were really heart-rending and I regretted very much that there was little I could do to help most of them.

A child who has lost a father writes and wants a man to talk to. A husband has deserted a family, and the mother and son both write. A young man trying to get in a service academy wants help. Pleas came from the ill, from orphans, and from people with little money.

My biggest regret in answering each of these letters was that we could not be of more help.

There have been situations that involved an exchange of letters—situations that have left me at a loss for words.

Sometimes nothing I could say seemed adequate, but I guess all of us have faced such times. The following letters labeled A, B, C, and D, and another group, E, F, and G, were exchanges of letters in such situations.

A

From a High-School Girl in New York

I admire you very much, especially your courage. I am writing to you for help and to tell you another story of courage.

I am 17 and a high school senior. Since the start of our senior year one of the boys in my class has suffered from cancer. At first he had two growths removed from his neck but at Christmas they found it had spread to his spine, and they operated to try to relieve some of the pain. He has been unable to walk. Now paralysis is setting in, and death is absolutely certain. He will not be able to return to school, and the pain is getting continuously worse. If you knew him you would never think this possible. John is so young, only 17, and he also had a very bright future. He was a Boy Scout, member of the National Honor Society throughout high school. He was one of our star basketball and baseball players and a loyal friend and classmate, always ready for fun. Only two weeks ago it was announced that he had received an appointment to the Air Force Academy. Last week it was also announced that he won a N. Y. State scholarship which he can never use. Now for the first time he is becoming discouraged. He has 2 older and 2 younger brothers and a younger sister. It is a very nice family. His father is City Judge, but his parents are there most of the time, his mother almost constantly.

Could you please try to help by writing to him. It might help his morale, maybe the other astronauts would too. Don't say that I asked you, *please*. Pray for a miracle. Thank you very much.

P.S. Don't tell anyone who wrote you. Thanks.

B

My answer:

Dear Patty:

Thank you very much for your letter of March 4. I guess the hardest type letter I ever have to answer is the type you sent, for I never know exactly what to say.

These things happen, and we don't know the reason. We are so used to reasoning things out and proving things by concrete methods in the laboratory or by experiment that we find it very hard to accept something as intangible as why someone such as John must go through what he is enduring. Many people tend to "blame" God for anything such as this that happens on the premise that "God gives and God takes away." I have never looked at it exactly that way. I feel that man is placed here with certain characteristics, talents, and capabilities, and left to a large degree on his own. Certainly God *can* control, but in thinking of this we reach a point which I certainly cannot explain, and beyond which we must just accept such a situation without letting it ruin our faith.

We never know what affect an individual life will have. For all we know, John may have accomplished more in his life to date, than many people do in 70 or 80 years. Our activities are so intertwined, that a chance remark or action may sometimes have a tremendous affect on someone else in his future endeavors. So even though John is young, the affect his life has had, or may have in the future, may be a great thing that we do not even foresee now.

I doubt if I have really helped any, but perhaps my above remarks can stimulate some thinking of your own in this regard. I certainly make no claim to know any more of the answers about such a situation than anyone else. I have so many questions in my own mind, that I really hate to try and advise anyone else in his thinking about such matters. But we don't know all the answers in this life, and there comes a time when we must accept what happens and still not let it affect what we believe. I very firmly believe that our short stay here on earth is but one phase of our existence and that we go on to greater things of which we now visualize little or nothing.

I have written a separate letter to John and trust that he will receive it about the same time as you receive this one. From your letter, I did not know exactly how much of the situation John, himself, was aware of. So my letter to him did not really express my feelings as much as this letter to you does. I will leave it up to your good judgment as to what you want to do with this letter, and if you think it can be of any advantage, please feel free to show this letter to John.

You sound like a pretty fine person yourself, Patty, to have written the kind of letter you did. My best regards to you.

C

My letter to John:

Dear John:

This morning I read a letter about courage—a story about a 17-year-old young man who is spending some of his Senior year in the hospital. That courageous fellow is you, John, and I wanted you to know how much I admire you. Your achievement of a scholarship to New York State and your appointment to the Air Force Academy indicate great accomplishments for which you can well be proud. I know for a fact that your fellow classmates look up to you as an example for them to follow in scholastic achievements, leadership ability, and personality traits.

It is difficult, I know, to lie in bed when you want to be working on your high-school projects. I am reminded of the story of Job in the Bible who not only lost everything he had in the way of material possessions, but also suffered much physical pain. Yet through it all he never once lost faith in God. His faith was well rewarded. Faith is a wonderful thing, John. It gives us an inward outlook that provides real security, and you have those kinds of faith and courage.

135

I have been told that you are interested in space projects, and I have enclosed some pictures and literature about the space program which I hope you will enjoy.

My very best regards to you, John.

D
Return Letter from Patty:

I'd like to thank you very much for your letter, it was really wonderful, and I can't thank you enough.

When I wrote to you at the beginning of March, we had no idea things would move so fast and I'm sorry but John died last Saturday the 16th. I thought John would really enjoy getting a letter from you and I'm still positive he would have. His parents read my letter and would like to thank you very much. Mr. _____ made a copy of it on his copying machine and I know I will always treasure mine. John's letter will be forwarded from Albany and I think they will get it tomorrow.

We knew it had to come, but nobody could quite believe it when it did. I guess we had sort of prayed for a miracle. I have enclosed the clipping from our newspaper. I thought you might like to read it.

To us John is and always will be a part of us. We are dedicating our yearbook in his memory. He was on the yearbook staff and worked very hard for it.

You have made many, many, friends through your letter and I'm sure the number will continue to grow. Very best of luck always.

E
From a Gray-Haired Grandmother in New Jersey

About six weeks ago, I was a passenger on an airplane out of Philadelphia. You also boarded at the same time.

You may recall sitting in the next seat forward, and you may also remember so kindly autographing my ticket envelope. That was the most thrilling part of my trip.

However, my big thrill did not last very long.

When I changed planes at Atlanta for Tampa, the ticket clerk kept this envelope and put my ticket in another one. I did not discover this till I began my trip home a week later.

I did so want to show your autograph to my son, who is a pilot.

Mr. Glenn, I would appreciate it so much if you would only autograph the enclosed slip of paper so I can always have something to remember one of the finest boys I ever met, and you may rest assured that no such mean person will ever get it again.

You may remember me as the little grayhaired grandmother who was seated just behind you.

I will appreciate this so much, and will always remember you.

F

From the Husband a Few Days Later

On Friday, November 23, I mailed a letter which my dear wife wrote you, concerning a stolen autograph which you so kindly gave her on a flight from Philadelphia to Washington. She was so proud and so anxious to show it to our son.

On that same day, at 1:15, our dear son met his death in an airplane crash enroute to Washington. The terrible shock has had such a terrible effect upon her that she is now unable to work.

We buried our boy yesterday. Colonel Glenn, I firmly believe that a word of comfort to her, over your signature, would do wonders to build up her courage and faith. This dear son was the only thing that kept her happy. We lost his brother fifteen years ago, a veteran of the entire Pacific ordeal.

Now we have no son.

Mr. Glenn, would you please give this note your kind consideration. Please know that we are not autograph hounds.

G

My answer:

Dear Mrs.—:

I certainly do remember you on that plane flight, and I thank you for the kind thoughts expressed in your letter.

A few days after I received your letter, I received a letter from your husband telling me of your son's death. You may well be proud of the service your son rendered his country. Our society has advanced steadily because of the contributions rendered by men such as your son.

At a time like this it is easy to lapse into feeling that we should blame God for something cut short of what we think it should have been. But it seems to me that rather than looking at it that way, we should be thankful for the happiness and the joy that we have been permitted to take part in, even though for a comparatively short time.

We never know the long-range effects or value that may accrue from a human life. Your son may have provided more blessings to others than some people will ever give, though they live to be 100.

At a time like this it is also comforting to know that what we may consider an end from our mortal viewpoint is only a beginning of something we all look forward to but cannot even envision now.

Please be assured that you have my heartfelt sympathy.

To Annie from a Widow in Florida

By means of TV, people who come into our homes, seem much like friends whom we have known for a long time.

Last Oct. I lay my husband to rest in Arlington National Cemetery.

I would like a wreath placed in front of the marker which I have never seen and a picture taken of it. If your time is available, kindly let me know, I will mail a wreath and check to reimburse you for trouble and expense.

I am unable to make a trip there at this time for I am caring for a 87 year old blind lady.

My comment:

Steve Grillo arranged to have a photographer take a picture of Annie laying the wreath at the grave. We sent the picture to this woman in Florida and subsequently received a wonderful letter of gratitude in return.

From a Woman in California

I am writing this in hopes there might be something you can do to help my younger brother get into the Air Force Academy.

After he took the exams they told him not to get his hopes up as there was very little chance of him getting in as only people with money and pull made the academies.

From a Girl in Ravenna, Ohio

I had red hair and freckles, too, and always hated my freckles until I found out you had them. Now I like them!!!

From a Boy in Jim Thorpe, Pennsylvania

Do you believe that science-fiction has, both directly and indirectly, influenced and advanced the coming, and the achievements of the space age?

You see, Col. Glenn, my parents are against my hobby of collecting science-fiction literature. They try to "tear it down", every chance they get, and threaten to burn my collection, because it is nonsense. Could you give me any advice on how to enlighten my parents on the facts about the virtues of science-fiction, because every way I have tried has failed since my father will not even listen when I try to explain.

They use the pretense that reading such literature will tend to influence me toward a "dream-world" life, and that it is responsible for my stuttering at present. I'm a stutterer, and this last summer I attended a speech program at State College, and my speech im-

139

proved tremendously, but I have to work on it constantly to keep it under control. Since I have come home I have gone back to my old pattern. And, just as the doctors stated, the harder I try to stop stuttering to please someone, the worst the blocks will become. But everytime I speak, my father stops what he is doing and stares at me critically and when I have a block, he gets angry and begins to yell. Because of this, I cannot hold eye contact with him when I speak to him, and eye contact is one of the first things I am to do in my program of getting control of my speech. I try to explain it to them, but right away, they simply tell me to keep quiet, because I don't know what I'm talking about. (After I've been a stutterer for about 9 years and had 12 weeks of intensive therapy.)

But, getting back to science fiction—I try to show interest in his hobbies of hunting (I even shot a deer this year), he never has, and will not show any interest in anything that I do. I'm on the football team, but he won't even go to the games, and when he does, all he has as comments are criticisms.

Can you give me any advice? I'd appreciate any help you can give me.

From a Lonely Young Boy in DeSoto, Missouri

I am only 10 years old. I have a problem, I am a only child and my parents both work. I don't have any friends that I am for sure that will be home when I call to see if they could come up and play. I thought you could give me some advice what to do when I don't have anyone to play with. I have plenty to do when it comes night time, but between the hours of 3 to 6 I usually don't have anything to do. So could you please try to give me some advice on what to do when I don't have anything to do.

From an Honest Young Girl in Birmingham, Michigan

About a week ago, I sent you a letter saying what a sharp kid I am. All I did was talk about myself, trying to earn a good name by you. I would like to make it up to you by telling the truth.

First and foremost, I am not 13, I am 12. Secondly I'm not vice-president of any eighth grade class, I'm just a nobody in the seventh-grade. I'm not even popular.

I was telling the truth about somethings, such as the fact that I am very fond of you.

I don't really know why I'm writing to you. I don't know if I'm writing just for the satisfaction of it or what. Maybe because I do love and admire you, and just can't stand decieving such an honorable man.

I know you think I'm crazy telling someone I love him when I haven't even met him. But somehow, when I'd watch you on TV and see you shakeing hands and talking to all those people, I'd get all choked up cause I wasn't there to see you, and somehow when you show that radiant grin of yours—well love is an emotion one cannot controll.

I do sincerely hope that you will forgive. I want you to with all my heart, for I do so want to earn your friendship.

P.S. Please write me a letter.

From a Woman in Florida

Please kindly help me if you can. I had a son and his birthday is April 16, and he was born April 16, 1925. But I didn't know my son was alive until last year in July. I tried in vain to find him, but he had his name changed, also adopted new parents and have everything fixed that nobody could find out who he is. I heard he knows all about me, and he is smart boy. I found out where he is, but I haven't got too much proofs. Please tell me what shall I do, go to my son and tell him or wait until I find out more about him. I don't have too long to live and I would like to see him and talk to him at least once before I die, or should I completely forget about him. Really Col. Glenn, its hard to do that. I cried every night wishing I could see him at least once. Maybe all seven astronauts could solve my problem.

141

From a Woman in Virginia

I don't know hardly how to write what I want to say in this letter. Well to get to the point, I have a lung condition, for going on two years now and am not well by no means. I was under the doctor a lot last summer and stayed eighteen days in the hospital just before Xmas. I had a lot of treatments but have paid out a lot for medicines and different things, but nothing has reached my trouble. I had X-rays made and the doctor said they showed asthma and pleurisy. I have had asthma all my life, but my chest hurts me so bad that I sometimes think that maybe the doctors are wrong as they are sometimes. I owe my doctor ninety-nine dollars and haven't paid him yet. We got behind and just didn't have it. I haven't been back to my doctor for a couple of months for that reason. I just go on day by day trying to hide my illness, but I know sooner or later something will take place and become serious if not already.

I am wondering if you and your friends as we are all your friends could help me that I might get better so I could continue to take care of my family. I have a husband and two children. We never know, some day I might be able to help you and yours at least you and yours have my prayer for health and happiness and success through the years to come.

From a Child Who Lost Her Father

I wish I had a father who was kind and loyal like you are. My father died 6 years ago this July. I was 7 and Marty was 2. We don't have many memories of daddy, but we will never forget him. He had cancer of the stomach. Lyn and Dave really must appreciate you, I would.

To My Daughter, Lyn

What I really wrote you for is to tell you how thankful I am that on the day of your father's orbits you were not griefstricken as I was late evening on November 30, 1961, when my father died. I am glad

142

that you don't have to find out the hard way what your father really means to you and what he means to the family pocketbook.

I hope your future social and school life is not effected in the wrong manner by your father's great success.

To Annie from a Mother

At times things get awful hard. You see, Mrs. Glenn, my husband deserted my little boy and I three years ago. I've prayed and so has my son, in fact he prays every night for his dad to come back. Since he left he has been in the hospital. He misses his Dad terrible and was very fond of him. I have a very good boy who goes to church, and prays and says grace at our meals. We have a home in Pa., but due to the lack of work we had to move to Md. My son watched your husband on TV and also went to D.C. to see him in the parade. He has all of the clippings and keeps up on space. He says he wants to be the first to go to the moon. He goes to D. C. every Sunday and spends the day in all of the famous buildings. He took a test for Military school. I think if he passes and I can afford it it will give him the religion he needs.

I am not putting a return address on this letter so if you don't get it, it won't come back. I don't want him to know I wrote to you. But if you see it in your power to answer this, please don't put your address on the outside.

From a Korean Student

How do you do Glenn sir.

We Korean and I congratulate you, your madam, your son, and your minister on your success.

I thinke so you have good remembering about Korean war. Just eleven years ago, the war made me one of numberous orphans.

Peace uncle Glenn

Today,

My necessity is only one,

It is school pay.

Would you mind helping me? If you can.

I want to become a Dr and a learned man.

If you help me with your mankaindship, I can help many other companies, with my faith and knwoladge.

I supplicate

you help me for my way and my dream.

good-bye dear uncle Glenn.

From a Wife in Hertfordshire, England

You and I had quite a day yesterday, you know what happened to you so I'll tell you what happened to me. I am a naval wife with four very young children. We are in the midst of moving from Scotland to our house in Hertfordshire. I got up and painted the drawing door then went to collect the milk and noticed that the removal van had knocked over two rose bushes belonging to our landlady. Whilst being helped by the gardener from the nextdoor house to replant the rose bushes, my two elder sons, age four & three, emptied the feathers out of a pillow all over my house and the newly painted door. Three hours later the phone rang (I had by this time gotten most of the paint & feathers off the door, and on to myself). It was my husband telling me to rush to the television set as you were just going to leave. Colonel Glenn, you weren't the only thing in orbit, my pressure cooker went up the same time as you did almost to the exact second.

Today I can laugh at yesterday, but please if any of you take off again do it in the middle of the night so that I can watch you in peace and with the knowledge my four year, three year, and eight month old sons plus my daughter who is just a year and eight months are tucked up in their beds.

"...CONSENT TO GIVE YOUR NAME TO...?"

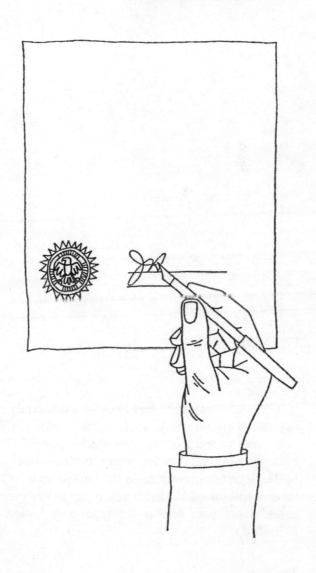

CHAPTER 9

The con artists and "fast buck" experts really have a field day following an event such as the orbital flight. Propositions have varied from the "borderline legal," through "fast buck promotional," to legitimate business offers from some of the largest corporations in the United States. One dubious scheme had me endorsing a new type kitchen utensil because it had seven uses just as the spacecraft I used was called Friendship 7.

The use of the name seemed to be the thing that most of the promoters wanted. Products to be named have varied from cigarettes, cigars, whiskey, and beer to products up to a foreign-make automobile that would have been named the "Glenn." Come to think of it, we never even discussed the performance characteristics of the "Glenn," but maybe that's a good thing.

Inventiveness in some people seems to express itself in others as a desire to write poetry or songs. There have been many hundreds of these poems and songs written since February, 1962. Some of them are good and some, well—. Other budding composers want me to get the songs or poems published for them. Others just want to present them as something they created that would be a nice memento or gift to indicate what they thought of the flight and of the following events.

Here are some excerpts that show the variety of these potential business ventures:

Our company is planning a special promotion to commemorate your mission. We would like to market astronaut pencils . . .

Should you be considering moving to a semi-rural area, we have a 172 acre tract under consideration for syndication and subdivision . . .

My judgement prompts me that you will make an excellent business associate. Therefore, I will appreciate it if you will arrange some time for me to meet you personally that I may explain my patent and idea to you . . .

We would like to produce a souvenir card honoring each astronaut and his achievements. We want to form a corporation to pay all expenses of advertising, production, legal fees, plus a percentage of profits to the astronauts . . .

I've been in the brokerage business for six months now and am rather short on customers. In case you decide to purchase securities you would open an account with me. If perhaps you and your family come to ———————, I would be most happy to line up accommodations and see that the city rolls out the red carpet for you . . .

At the present time I am unemployed and feel I can make a few dollars with these cups and give the Americans something that they will keep forever. I don't know how to approach this matter. I do feel that the answer will come from you astronauts . . .

So sorry to hear of your fall in the bathroom. I would like you and your wife to have a pair of non-skids . . .

I have been led by the spirit of God to ask you for a donation for my church . . .

I write to suggest you build some efficiencies for us older people for around 60 to 70 a month.

Enclosed is a copy of a government royalty free patent which may be of interest to you . . .

And here are some longer suggestions:

Amsterdam, 23 rd of March 1962

To Mr. John Glenn,
<u>ARLINGTON U.S.A.</u>

Dear Mr. Glenn,

At first I will congratulate you with your achievement
and as a token of esteem I request your consent to give
your name to a little firm I want to establish.

The name of the <u>firm will</u> be after your consent

      HANDELSONDERNEMING " GLENN "

My decision to give your name to my firm is taken
out of respect for your enormous achievement.

I hope you will give your permission and I meanwhile
remain,

                Yours faithfully,

M. Bos,   M. Bos
Stolwijkstraat 4 '''
<u>AMSTERDAM.</u>
The Netherlands.

From a Woman in Cincinnati, Ohio

I am sending an interesting clipping I hope is of value to you. If it is of value to you, please return $3.00.

Newspaper clipping:

ASTRONAUT JOHN GLENN was welcomed home to New Concord to the strains of "When Johnny Comes Marching Home," but he almost wasn't.

Two nights before the celebration, Mrs. Sara Henritzy of 8775 Old Indian Hill road, casually remarked to her husband, Owen, that she had meant to drop New Concord a note about the perfect welcoming song. Owen, a phone company engineer, placed a call to New Concord's Mayor James Taylor and then handed her the phone.

"Ohimgost—it's a must!" said Mayor Taylor. "With all the musical suggestions we've had, nobody thought of it."

And that's how Johnny Glenn came marching home, in a convertible, of course.

From a Cigar Manufacturing Company in Switzerland

To honour your name we would very much like to hear whether you would allow us that we give one of our brands your name. For your information we have the license to produce the famous Churchill cigars in Switzerland. We would very much like to add to this the "Captain Glenn" brand.

From a New York Inventor and His Wife

I never under estimate a women's intuition, that is, my wife's which is the reason why I am addressing this to both of you.

I was blessed with an inventive mind, parts of my ideas have been put in use.

Now, I have come up with another item, which I would like to see developed and produced in large quantities, but like the others, it is too big for me to handle alone. I need competent help.

The item is a fire fighting apparatus, which in synchronized function will break small or large oil tank fires, atomic bombing fires, earthquake fires and forest fires at the rate of a SQUARE MILE *a minute. Utilizes solids or water. The latter would not present any problems, anywhere.*

It is fantastic, as much as orbiting the earth would have been in the preceding century.

From a Poet in Wisconsin

If you publish my poem, will you please send me a copy?

THE PULSE OF SPACE

Hats off! to our man of space
Gallant symbol of our race.
You, JOHN GLENN, we all admire
For your spirit and your fire.
You, who dared the universe,
A man with a mission great
Planned through by man, defied fate
Collecting data, this, for real
Paved the future, with true zeal.

From an Ambitious Author in the State of Washington

I have sent you under separate cover a copy of my latest Novel which I hope you will enjoy reading same as my friend Sir Winston.

If you will be kind enough to send me a few lines over your own signature giving me your impressions and approval I shall be glad to

*give you in return half of my earnings from the sale of the books,
the TV rights, and other sources. This will mean many thousands
of dollars. With your indorsement it is bound to go over in a big
way, because you are now sitting on the top of the world and it will
pay you to cash in on your popularity.*

From a Woman in Kansas

I don't know whether you might be interested in becoming a silent
partner in a business that has a gross of around $88,000 yearly, but
I need someone who can invest $1,800 for ⅓ of the profits.

It is a feed and grain business and would net around $45,000
yearly. I would need the money within 12 days.

I've never had much money and very few of the things I've
wanted, but I'm divorced and have a 5-year old son to care for.

The profit from this business would result in being able to repay
my debts, help my father after he retires early in May, to go to
Europe and to remarry.

From a Man in Florida

I myself am offering you the chance to come in with me on my
new invention which looks and resembles the capsule you rode in,
and it is a utensil for the housewife and homemakers to use when
baking. If you come in with me you would make an honestly
earned Million Bucks. This utensil can perform 7 different chore's
for the homemakers. And where it does 7 different things. If I am
not mistaken your capsule was No 7 and believe me this little utensil
will always be in the homes to always be seen by all people. They
(*continued on page 154*)

152

478 E. 9th Street
Brooklyn 18. N.Y.
May 3rd, 1964

Dear Colonel Glenn:

On Feb 20th, 1962 I wrote the following poem:

John H. Glenn, Jr
World Traveler

J ust a picture of spaceship way up in the sky
O ccupied by John Glenn - a world-famous "guy"
H e reached the heights and flew around the earth
N ow his record is hailed in the land of his birth.

H ow many hours, days, months and years

G iven by him to this project of all hemispheres
L ogging each rehearsal for the ultimate day
E verything was finally called A-OKAY?
N ationally, inter-nationally, his fame is assured
N ow, the full triumph for the stress he endured.

J oin with me in the tribute to Colonel John Glenn
R enowned, now and forever, with the bravest of men.

When you find time please write me as I have some ideas of nationwide benefit which could be developed by you as an individual of great prestige, and would help your state of Ohio, in particular.

Sincerely,
Robert Irwin Lite

will not have to open a History Book to be reminded of your famous ride in your capsule because the housewife will always be using it and it will always be in plain view for everybody to see at all times. I'll even go so far as to sell it to you outright with all patent rights to it. It's a fortune for you and not for me. I soon will die from a heart ailment.

P.S. I am old enough to be your father. So this will prove to you that I do not write letters for fun or like a screw ball, excuse the word.

"MAY I HAVE YOUR...?"

CHAPTER 10

From a Young Lady in New York

I am thirteen years old, and I think your son Dave is a doll. Would you please send me a picture of him.

To Annie from a Housewife in New York

I am making a wool-braided rug (10′ × 15′) for my living-room. Many of my friends have given me old wool clothing to use in it. Would you please send me an old wool scarf, shirt, or something worn-out of your husband's that I could use in my rug.

From a Couple in California

We collect elephant bric-a-brac. At the present we now have 194 of them from different parts of the world. Would you please, at your most convenient time send us one with your autograph? They may be found at any 5 & 10 store.

From a Scouting Executive in Missouri

As an added incentive in our ticket sales among the boys, I am inquiring into the availability of an autographed picture of yourself in your space suit. If the pictures would be available, we would need approximately 500.

From a Young Man in New York

I hope you can do a little favor for me. Remember the lapel pin you gave your nephew shaped like a Capsule. If it were possible would you please send me one like that.

P.S. I would be very glad to own a pin that John Gleen gave me. Thank you very much.

A Public Relations Officer from England Writes:

The committee have suggested that perhaps you would be kind enough to loan us, for this Exhibition, your helmet as an exhibit of interest. We are showing a Blue Streak Rocket, together with a Rolls Royce Jet Engine, and we feel that your helmet would create great interest, particularly amongst the younger members of the Association. You can be assured that great care would be taken of this helmet.

A Young Student from Ohio Writes:

Our English teacher told us to write to some famous person and to ask him what his favorite poem was. I almost instantly decided to write and ask you. So can you please tell me what your favorite poem is and why?

157

A Young Boy from Texas Writes:

Would you please send me some rocket wire about 65 feet and a picture of you. I would like that very much.

A Young Boy from Pennsylvania Writes:

Could you please send me some of the man-made banana pellets that NASA feed to the monkeys that NASA sends up in space?

From a Member of the Illinois Egg Council

Astronaut Glenn, I know it would be impossible for you to attend a breakfast which the Illinois Egg Council is giving in honor of Governor Kerner of Illinois. Would it be possible to have a picture of you—eating breakfast or otherwise. We could have it enlarged and in this way we could include you in our event.

From a High-School Senior in New Jersey

We should like to reproduce on the divider pages of our yearbook short handwritten letters from famous Americans, telling the importance that they place on public school education.
We should like very much to use a letter from you.

From a Man in Arizona

I'm writing to you as a serious collector of autographs, very much anxious to obtain a genuine bit of your handwriting.

It is my hope that I might receive a personal letter from you, perhaps even entirely in your own hand, rather than a signed typewritten one. And/or a photograph of yourself, personally inscribed to me.

From Three Schoolboys in Massachusetts

Please send us one of those Colonel Glenn banners, so we may put it up with our school banners.

From a Child in Michigan

Give me your picture. Bye.

From a Young Lady

I am wondering whether you might know of someone at the Cape who might be interested in corresponding with me.

From a Woman in Florida

Our sorority is planning a celebrity Hat Sale for the 15th of March. Would you be kind enough to send us one of your hats for this sale?

A Man from New York Writes:

Enclosed find the luncheon menu of the Waldorf Astoria "Hero's Welcome". I would appreciate very much if you would autograph the luncheon menu.

From a Quilting Enthusiast in Michigan

I would appreciate it very much if you would honor me in signing the enclosed quilt block.

A Sunday School Teacher from North Carolina Writes:

I need one of your old shoes. My theme in the talk to the young people will be the young people of today will have to fill these shoes tomorrow.

A West Pakistan Boy Writes:

Dear Uncle Glenn,

How are you. I am a student of Pakistan and I am very much interested in space flights. I congratulate you on your successful flight around the world. My age is about 15 years. What is the name of your son and daughter. I want to know their names, because I want to make friendship with my letter soon.

Can you do one things, that is, take autograph's of all American Spacemen including yours, which is very precious over here to be find. Please Uncle reply soon. Now I am closing the letter and goodbye to Auntie Glenn and your son and daughter.

160

A Fourteen-Year-Old Boy from Canada Writes:

I am . . . Belgium boy who wrote you already 2 times asking you for one photograph with an autograph.

I even sent you a dollars bill for the expense, but I guess that you don't care for a litle 14 years boys, because you didnt' answer, you may keep the monay (monay that I save for that purpose) as souvenir from a naive disappointed boy who trusted you in vain.

In case you change your mind, here is my address.

From Seniors Planning a
High-School Beauty Contest in Georgia

Approximately eighty beauty pictures will be made in October and, if you accept [to be a contest judge], will be sent to you. When the annuals have been completed, you will receive one as our token of appreciation.

To Annie from a High-School Teacher in Vermont

Knowing that my pupils do not eat a good breakfast I am emphasizing the importance of starting the day out right with a wholesome breakfast. It is my aim to do a bulletin board of a typical breakfast of famous people. Would you please send me a typical breakfast of your husband's. That should impress my 8th grade boys, as they all aspire to be astronauts.

161

From a Father in New Jersey

The enclosed strip of tape adorned the skies over New York City on March 1, 1962 on the occasion of Colonel John Glenn's momentous reception here. Please autograph the enclosed tape.

From a Girl in Bennettsville, South Carolina

Would you please send me a picture of you. Do you like to twist?

From an Eleven-Year-Old New Yorker

I'm eleven years old. I watched your launch on TV. I was praying for you and I see my praying and everybody else's praying came true. Getting down to facts, I would like to know if you could send me one autographed picture of yourself.

From a Church Group in Illinois

Because of your own Christian witness, we feel your autograph to be highly appropriate in the Bibles. We would like to have your permission to send two Bibles to be autographed by you.

162

From a Man in Ohio

My hobby is the history of old time barber shops & barbers, also barber shop items. Would it be asking too much if I were to ask you for the razor that you used when you shaved the morning before you took this space flight?

From a Man in Missouri

I am asking for your permission to addressing this letter and for your kindness to autograph for me the enclosed two covers. One bearing 4c Project Mercury block of 4 stamps with your picture. One Airship "Hindenburg" already autographed by Orville Wright, Amelia Earhart and Dr. Eckener the airship commander in this flight.

To President John F. Kennedy
from a Young Man in Connecticut

Dear Mr. President:
I would like to have an autigraph of you and, John Glenn, and one hair of you and Glenn.

From a Children's Orthodontist in Nebraska

If it would be possible for you to be so kind as to send me an autographed photograph with a suitable caption such as, "Healthy teeth and strong bodies make better astronauts." I think it would have a tremendous psychological effect on my patients.

From a Grandmother in Ohio

Well, here is my problem. Will you give your consent to another John Glenn, the Astronaut? You see, I say to him (grandson), "You mean you want to be an Astronaut," and each time, he replies, "No, grandma, I'm going to be John Glenn, the Astronaut." As you know, it takes a little time to have your name changed in the courts, and we thought we had better begin now, so as to achieve this goal in time for him to be John Glenn, the Astronaut.

Are you willing to share your name, or what do you propose we do?

YOU CAN'T WIN 'EM ALL

CHAPTER 11

No matter what is done there are always a few people who want to criticize, tell how to do it better, or just complain that it's being done at all. Some offer very sincere suggestions because they are truly concerned. Some may have a mental quirk or two that lead to an extravagant or ridiculous statement or assumption, but others are just chronic complainers who would find something wrong with anything.

From a Man in Newport, Kentucky

Dear Mr. Kenidy Presadent
Of the USA i Own A Rooming House and I have noticed that since Mr Glen ho orbited the Earth 3 times has caused so much impurity in the Air that every One in this House has bin coffing and snoting i believe that this kind of stuf should bee stoped as it causes the Air to bee soo impure it causes this trouble i think some-

thing should bee don to stop these impurities in the Air after all your Life and Mine is more importent than sending this impurity into the Air after all the Air is not pure like when i was 15 years old i will bee 77 years the 30th of April this Year and i think the Air was much Purer when iwas a Boy wee should do something about this

Copy of Newspaper Clipping Attached to Letter

> "WATCH FOR. . . . *The father of Astronaut John H. Glenn, Jr. to appear in Chicago's St. Patrick's day parade. The senior Mr. G. is a plumber. Steve Bailey of the Chicago Journeymen Plumbers, local 130, is extending the invitation."*

Please do not tear down the beautiful life your illustrious son, Col. John Glenn displayed during the past few weeks. He stands for all that is good and am sure would not approve of his father showing off in an Irish St. Patrick Day parade whether in Chicago or any other city. You are Protestants and a fine American family, so do not join the Irish Catholics in a parade of Non-Protestants. Bless you all.

An Unsigned Note

Glad you got back safe but do you know your trip was a sin. God made people for the earth—not the sky or the moon. I don't care what your minister said.

They are making an idol of you. That is pagan. Look in the Bible where God confused the tongues of people because they wanted to build a tower to heaven. It is idol worship. If that's what you want —O. K. You will answer to God.

From a Family in Concord, North Carolina

Now, let me tell you the real reason for writing you this letter. Yes, to congratulate you for one reason, but for another, to tell you how disappointed we were in you after the flight. So many times before your flight, we read the statement that you were a very religious man, having much faith in God. There were also a number of pictures of you going to church. All this gave us a very good impression of the man we were "sold on."

Now, what was the disappointment? Well, after the miraculous flight, we failed to hear or read a statement of your thanking God or giving God credit for anything you had accomplished. We're sure that there are thousands of families all over the United States that felt this same disappointment as we did. Maybe you did give God "thanks" secretly, we hope and pray that you did. But don't you think it would be nice if you let the world know that God was head of that "team" you spoke of so admiringly in your news conferences concerning your success?

We pray to God for your continued success.

From an Anonymous Correspondent

As we look at this crazy world today and wonder what the abnormal demented sadistic mind man will do next he has dared to penetrate Gods elements and he is indeed to be feared and should be in a straight jacket and behind locked doors. What kind of ministers do we have today such as yours is that would sanction such a terrifying act. If Almight God wanted man to touch the elements he would of put them within man's reach. You almost lost your life in this last horrifying episode as men have no right to touch God's elements and your religious outlook on all this money making so called space mess is one word money and God in his time will destroy evil men who wont mind their own business. No one in their right mind would ever think of doing what you and the others did. We are the laughing stock of the whole world using tax money to beat God. You were fool enough to let yourself be used. No one but demented fiends would attempt to fight God and his elements so stop fighting as you wont win. When these crazy sadists try you the more God will be ready for them with fire and brim stone and it will be a pleasure to see you come down a flaming torch.

A real Christian who still believes in letting God's world alone.

From a Man in Mississippi

As we traveled along a Texas highway in our earth-bound vehicle, listening by radio to your speech to Congress, we hoped and prayed you would not overlook one person who has been so long forgotten; the one person upon whom depends all progress; and who has been plodding along, doing his share without any apparent recognition from any source. That person is the American taxpayer. The old fellow would have been so happy if you had only mentioned his name on this historic occasion. He would have given you his last shirt.

Colonel Glenn, you represent all the people who had any part in the success of your historic flight. We salute you.

Another Man from Mississippi

Thought you might be interested in this unpopular opinion.

With all regard for the dedication, discipline, and genuine interest you have shown in the Space efforts, I must tell you that I think our emphasis is terribly misplaced.

We have *chronic* and ever-growing problems, *on earth,* problems of security and dignity which are being avoided and bungled.

The organized and scientific approach (so imperative to Space programs) is in no way applied to our problems of privation, in justice, or inequities.

However, I am glad you are back in Ohio.

Good luck,

From a Woman in Rockville, Maryland

If the moon should break up the earth would probably be better off, not worse. Whence the necessity to try sticking to a stellar body without an atmosphere and with hardly any gravity? Suppose a man managed to do it for a while before he died, what good would the little he learned be to anyone on earth?

Yet you ask us to pay for it, while the hopes that children may have been able to sprout are blasted, and they and many grown-ups, disillusioned and thwarted, become delinquents, or leading criminals, to be reckoned with in the halls of our elected legislators and elected executives. If that is not insanity, what is?

169

To: The President
of the United States of America
Re: Orbit Around the World

Kindly allow me to suggest to you at this day and hour that the man selected for this dangerous mission is no longer suitable on the grounds that repeated delays have shot this brave man's nerves to pieces. The man is not yet built who can take all that Glen has endured and still be in top health condition.

I sincerely urge, Sir, that the #2 man should be told at the last moment (to save undue tension) to enter the capsule to ensure a greater chance of success.

Trusting the endeavors of our Nation will meet with wonderful success.

From a Woman in Homestead, Florida

You do not know me. But like millions of Americans, I knew you as a hero desperately needed by an America which is sick of dishonor and dishonorable men.

Your great feat, your faith in God, your simplicity and modesty made all of us stand a little taller and gave us pride in being Americans. You were a patriot in the American tradition—a man to whom we could point our children. And then, the exploiters and the opportunists moved in.

At first, we were uneasy as we saw the crowding into the limelight, the attempted identification with and the exploitation of the public's great esteem for you. Then we were saddened as the image began to tarnish—as an American hero blurred into a water skier, a Washington playboy and finally a political pawn to bring new lustre to a shoddy machine.

We feel cheated, Colonel. We feel that all America has lost something precious. We need great men to look up to, to measure up to. It is still true today that "without vision, the people perish . . ."

We wish that you could find the courage to return to duty. Our country needs you.

"NOW THAT YOU'VE ENTERED POLITICS..."

CHAPTER 12

For a number of reasons which were adequately reported in the press, I made the decision in early 1964 to announce my candidacy for the U. S. Senate from the State of Ohio. This evoked mixed emotions in many people and was reflected in their letters. Thoughts seemed to polarize—those definitely for and those very definitely against such action. Where politics were involved, it was amazing that most people seemed to have little middle ground. They were either 100 per cent for the action I was taking or 100 per cent against it. Unfortunately, I had an accident in Columbus, Ohio, on February 26th, 1964, which left me with injuries that would require a number of months for recovery, and the doctor strongly advised me to withdraw from the Senatorial race. This I did, but some of the letters prior to the withdrawal make an interesting commentary on our political life.

Many people, without knowing me personally, or having considered my reasons for trying to take this means of rendering further service to the country, made many erroneous assumptions concerning my motives, and seemed to be quite at home doing this simply because the subject was politics. This could, and probably should, be the subject of further discussion or writing at a later date.

A Pennsylvania Veteran Writes:

You have an exalted position in the minds of all Americans, and I was sorry to hear of your going into politics some time ago.

Because—in my estimation—a politican is a hypocrite, a liar, a back-stabber and a moral crook. He has to be in order to keep on being a politician, and get elected.

Servicemen's Mothers from Massachusetts Write:

You belong in Service, you have plenty of important things to do for our Flag than joining Politics.

You would be lost to us as a Senator, possibly not get it anyway and be out a Army to boot.

Politics is only for men who can't do anything real but talk their heads off.

Your real, you are highly respected and admired by the young, don't spoil it with politics.

From a Mother in Michigan

Really, how could you!?

I greatly admired your feat in space and your American ideals —until you "fell for the Kennedy play" and into their swimming pool.

And now you are running for the senate—as a Democrat! Where have your principals gone?

A Woman from Georgia Writes:

You are a prime example of the type of American President Kennedy was referring to when he said, "Ask not what your country can do for you, but ask what you can do for your country."

173

A Woman from California Writes:

Your sincerity, patriotism, and eagerness to share your fame with all the other people responsible for the success at your flight are wonderful traits.

Your decision to "enter politics" pleased me personally because I consider public service one of the finest professions. America needs devoted citizens like you to serve her.

It's not a question of whether or not you could win an election. The big question is: if elected, will you be a good senator? Don't you honestly feel that a U. S. Senator should have some experience in government and law before becoming a Senator?

I hope you will withdraw from the Senate campaign and make plans to enter politics some other way—as a city Director, County Supervisor, or even on the state level.

From a Man in Pennsylvania

Please keep your priceless "image" as it is now. You were only being used, on a national scales by a ruthless machine.

Anonymous

You were smart to quit the idea of running for Senate as you would never have won.

A Housewife from Massachusetts Writes:

Get that library card busy and become an expert on the subject. Study especially the wheeling-dealing that you must do. I imagine that this is really the most difficult part for an honest man. We need men like you in the Senate.

A Supporter of My Opponent,
A Minister from Ohio Writes:

Thus to forsake the space age program of our country. That was the field where your experience meant much to this nation and to the American people. But now you have turned your back on it all. I do sincerely hope that you have carefully thought it all over and that the patriotic motivation is deeply laid in your own mind.

In the first place you are possessed of no experience in the political field; you should have remained in the area where your ability as a leader was quite advanced.

I have talked with perhaps a dozen different citizens the past few days and all of them have attitudes similar to mine. They will oppose you politically. They feel that you have let them down miserably.

You would have done better had you accepted a spot in the lower political regions and worked yourself up from stage to stage toward a higher ranking within your party. The average citizen thinks that you judge yourself too highly as justifying your advancement by one big leap to a high spot in American political life.

Now I say it without rancor and with all due respect for you and your career. I hope that Mr. Young trounces you badly and that, if he does not thus beat you, that Mr. Taft, and upcoming statesman from Ohio, will snow you under in the coming election in November. The people will now measure you as a politician and not as a space hero. I will do everything I can to bring about your defeat.

From an Eighty-Year-Old Texan

Does your heroic and successful effort in your chosen field make you an authority in All??

I know you've been asked "Are you being considered for future Vice President?" John stop it—Five different men were promised the Vice Presidency in 1960 Democrat convention Nomination. If their states delegation would come as solid vote for Kennedy —what states—Michigan Minnesota—Kansas, Iowa—I'll make your governor Vice President. Washington State—I'll make your Senator Vice President. Forgive me John—truth is sometimes ugly—Stick to your "Aeronauting Job."

175

A Political Plan from New Mexico

You would be an outstanding President—When reports came out that Bud Wilkenson might file for the Senate race I thought what a fine team this would be.

You would have to run on an independent ticket, but this is no problem.

The Republicans are not coming up with any one who could win and the Democrats are going to be better over civil rights.

Mr. Kennedy started a trend toward youth and you and Bud would fit into this picture and benefit greatly from it.

Complete honesty and simplicity, avoiding any debates or saying one word against the opponents.

From a Woman in Maryland

Your qualifications as an astronaut hardly qualify you for the Senate! Although your education may not be sufficient to have given you such inright into American Public life, you must have some notion that being a physical specimen for NASA does not make you a statesmen.

Your opponent in the primary is a proven, loyal Democrat for registered voters like us, this counts more than all the gall you bring to your campaign.

I hope Senator Young beats the hell out of you.

A Man from Virginia Writes:

Having to withdraw from the political mill in Ohio may have been a sharp disappointment for you, but it may be best in the sight of God. In the eyes of America you represent something more precious than politics, I feel certain. This is not to belittle the importance of politics but rather to accent the values of the spirit which people see in you.

176

From a Staunch Supporter

They say you're too nice a guy to get mixed up in politics. You haven't enough experience. You are motivated by ulterior reasons. Mustn't disturb the status quo.

No one seems the least bit concerned with whether or not you would make a good senator. I happen to think you would, and that reason is the last link in a chain of reasons why I intend changing my registration from Republican to Democrat. A chain that began with Franklin Rooseveldt, incidentally.

I happen to believe you will represent me better than anyone else could, and I would ask that more people re-examine that word "represent". I do not mean that you would do the most for me. That is patronage, not representation. The man who would best represent me is the man who would be most likely to vote as I myself would vote on critical issues. That I think you would do.

Senator Young seems to feel that a continuous record of always voting with the White House entitles him to some sort of perpetuity in office.

If it be so vital that our man in Washington always vote according to White House dicta, wouldn't it be simpler, and one devil of a lot cheaper, to send a rubber stamp?

You are going to be hurt, little pal, before this is over. You and your wife and your parents. You will be abused and villified and insulted and lied about. You will be made to appear dishonest, arrogant, and only slightly less stupid than the village idiot. And you will reach the point where you wonder if it is worth it. And I hope that when things are the blackest, you will hunt out this small token of my great esteem, read it thoughtfully, and know that at least one person wants you for his representative, and is working for you, praying for you, and in the final count-down, voting for you.

A Woman from Pennsylvania Writes:

I have always been of the opinion that you had to be a little bit crooked to be in politics, so I am certainly looking forward to the day when you're in there pitching with your high standards, it will certainly make for a better government.

177

From a Woman Who Gave No Address

I want to tell you that your decision to enter the political field is one that will, I am sure, meet with the whole hearted approval of many people.

What matters is that you believe in your country and it's future. I do not think it is necessary and have been active in politics all one's life in order to acquire an interest or ability in the affairs of government.

I feel you have the necessary spiritual and moral courage to do this—just as you had the physical courage required for your launch into space.

I believe we need men such as you in the government—men who are dedicated to their country's greatness—men of courage and wisdom and vision.

The inspiration that he was around the world must not be allowed and dissipate—that is why we need men of your calibre in the government. If he had been given time the lost leader (Kennedy) might have said to us

"To you with failing hands we throw the torch
  Be yours to hold it high
  If ye break faith with us who die, We shall not sleep"

I believe that you, with your qualities, can hold that torch high—can help it "light the world."

From a Sixth-Grade Student in New York

If I were 21 I'd vote for you with no hesitation.

From a Twelve-Year-Old Ohioan

I'm very disgusted to also hear that you are not going for Senate.

I think you would make a good senator although I would not vote for you. You may wonder why I will not vote for you. The reason why is because I'm a twelve years old boy.

A Grandfather from Michigan Writes:

Politics is not a clean profession. Your people will say a lot of things to make you unhappy—your best friends will say and do mean things for personal gains. God did not intend for one man to conquer the world.

Please stay with your family—and wait to play with your grandchildren like me some day then you will be more happier. I have 4 grandchildren and again I say stay out of politics—I don't think you need money that bad.

If you wish write me a short note—let me know what you think.

An Ardent Democrat from Spokane, Washington, Writes:

The Republican was afraid the Democrat had a to good man in you—and they, we had a good man in you—too, and we still have—so go to it—Demand and Command—tell Our dear God—Do it to day, do it to stay, do it Gods way.

A Suggestion to President John F. Kennedy
from a Virginian

Why not give this country a good bit of publicity, just like Russia did only more so. Why not send Colonel Glenn around the world with movies of his trip and show it to the people around the world. This is something that Russia can't do because just between you and me I don't think they ever sent anyone around the world that is living.

179

A Retired Serviceman from Nevada Writes:

You seem to have run into a hazard we hadn't anticipated when we set up that survival course for you some years ago. We covered practically everything but a slippery bathroom floor; maybe we should crank this additional environmental danger into the curriculum.

I am sorry that you have withdrawn from the senate race; you have some qualities that are spectacularly lacking in many members of that august body: guts, intelligence and integrity. I find myself quite often in contempt of congress these days; if it were not for jeopardizing my retirement pay I would be tempted to agitate a revolution to change the system.

The myth of wise old age has practically throttled both houses, it seems to me. Charlie Wilson once said that he couldn't see where giving a general another star made him any smarter, and in some cases this is true. The same thing applies to adding another year to a man's age: they just don't get any smarter as they grow older. I say this from the pinnacle of my sixty years. If a guy hasn't got it at forty he aint never going to have it.

Some of those ossified old dodos in congress have, simply by virtue or outliving other men, consolidated themselves in positions of power all out of proportion to their individual merit. When one obstinate old bastard with a mind right out of the last century can block legislation that a majority wants, it seems to me to be time for a change. Maybe a limit of two terms, as has been recently suggested, is the answer.

I wish you a speedy recovery and better luck on the next go round.

A Bostonian Writes:

Our senate, Congress, state and local governments are in dire need, not of trained politicians but of disciplined men. You then, are eminently qualified for the position which you sought. You have been trained in many disciplines. Moral discipline, a man who was not afraid to proclaim his faith in God. Military discipline, the discipline of flying, quick judgements, instant decisions. The discipline of science and of mathematics and finally the discipline of the astronauts training program.

Rest assured that many Americans are praying for your complete recovery.

They look forward to seeing the John Glenn grin in the halls of the Capitol and his pilots' hands at the wheel of legislative progress.

Three High-School Girl Campaigners Write:

. . . but the disappointment was not as hard to bear when we thought what we were doing. Some people just talk about their government and don't do anything to help it, but we feel that just by the small things we did in your headquarters, we have become more informed and better citizens and future voters. We sincerely want to thank you for this wonderful opportunity.

My comment:

These are three fine dedicated young ladies who worked in our campaign headquarters for a time. The "thanks" is going the wrong way here. I thank you, girls, for the opportunity to know and represent you.

A Lawyer from Oregon Writes:

This is written in regretfulness, not resentment: and indeed, an American were an ingrate who should resent any decision by so superior a fellow countryman as you, and one whom we owe much.

To a quivering scaredy cat like me, it is incomprehensible how men of your stripe, displaying two years ago an horizon of laughing courage beyond naming shrink away from standing up against the bandwagon of the more-government party, when you enter the commonplace of the rialto and leave it to us who lack sand: it plain beats me how that can be but it is.

I can only extend my hopes that you lose the nomination to more-government Young—and then feel no sorrow at his loss to Less government Taft; so that I can once again be,
                                        Yours Respectfully

A Woman from Illinois Writes:

I decided this day must not pass until I wrote and told you how delighted I am that you have entered the political arena. Also I'm delighted you chose my beloved Democratic Party.

Young man, your going to be President of the United States someday.

For goodness sake, pay no attention to those who accuse you of trying to captilize on your being a national hero.

A Young Student from Ohio Writes:

My parents were very disappointed when they heard you would not be able to run in the Ohio May fifth Primary.

Not too long ago I saw your wife on television. I thought it was wonderful for her to campaign for you while you were recovering.

My comment:

I agree. While I was in the hospital, Annie and Rene Carpenter campaigned for me in Ohio and were doing a wonderful job. So good, in fact, that I think either one of them would have made good candidates themselves. After my withdrawal, I still received over 205,000 votes and I jokingly told Rene and Annie I felt the source of the support was probably 100,000 for Rene, 100,000 for Annie, and 5,000 for me.

"I KNOW WHAT
YOU'RE GOING THROUGH…"

CHAPTER 13

I mentioned earlier that in February, 1964, I had an accident in which I fell and struck the left side of my head. This caused some difficulty with the balance mechanisms near my left ear, and left me very sensitive to head motions. I was in the hospital for two months and then spent a long recuperation period at home. Many people misread my condition, believing it to be something other than simply the result of a fall, such as an infection, or a connection with space flight.

My trouble was very simple, I slipped on a throw rug on a slick bathroom floor while adjusting a heavy mirror and fell, striking my head against the side of the bathtub. It was strictly a contact injury, having no connection with space flight. Incidentally, I had never experienced any periods of dizziness prior to the injury even under the stress of the orbital flight.

There are many difficulties that can occur with the balance mechanism of the inner ear—the labyrinth—and many of these are generally termed "labyrinthitis." One type of labyrinth difficulty can be caused by a blow on the head, such as I received. Another type of labyrinthitis is that caused by an infection, from a variety of causes, and is known as Meniere's disease. Since the Meniere's symptoms are similar to those from a blow on the head such as I had, many people reading of my symptoms assumed that I shared their difficulty with Meniere's disease.

There is nothing, apparently, that draws people more closely together than being fellow-sufferers with the same type of ailment. And I can assure you that when these people wrote to me of their sympathy, their own symptoms, experiences, and treatments, I in turn could sympathize with them, for in many cases we did apparently have very similar feelings.

The treatments suggested were those that had been individually effective for other people, but one thing I might add is that labyrinthitis can be treated by a whole host of drugs and treatments. Individual reaction seems to be a matter of wide variance and what will work satisfactorily for one person may not work for another. In my case, I just needed rest and time for the congested area around the left labyrinth to reabsorb. There are just no treatments that can speed up that slow process. I am happy that my recovery has been 100 per cent even though it took most of a year to accomplish the whole recovery process.

Any of the suggestions that appeared to have some merit I gave to my doctors and there were suggestions that had merit. My doctors investigated these thoroughly and made notes for future use, even though the remedies didn't apply to my case. Other suggestions, as you will see, were not so seriously considered.

One of the most interesting letters among the latter category has been misplaced and is not included in the following chapter. It was from a man who went into great detail about the vertigo and dizziness symptoms he had experienced, how horrible they were, how much he had suffered and of how many thousands of dollars he had spent going to three different well-known major clinics. He ended up with the doctors telling him that there was nothing to do but just learn to live with his problem. This he did for a year, but it was very aggravating and it was difficult to go to work every morning. He said that one morning he was so disgusted with the whole program that he just stopped and had two big shots of whiskey from his liquor cabinet before he left the house. He said that in a matter of minutes all the symptoms were gone and he felt fine. He reported that this is a daily routine now. That he has been doing this for ten years—two shots of whiskey every morning before he goes to work and his problem has been solved. He strongly recommended that I use the same treatment. I didn't have the heart to tell him that he wasn't cured but had probably just been partially drunk for the last ten years.

Most of the letters, however, were just very heartfelt expressions of concern and commiseration that one soul feels for another when he has endured the same troubles.

A quick sampling reads remarkably like a small digest of American folk medicine:

. . . I was warned never to look up. Now it doesn't bother me but I am partially deaf . . .

. . . You must get in touch with Dr. ——. He performs an operation behind the ear and inserts a plastic tube that somehow carries away the moisture that drains into the inner ear that causes the unbalanced attack . . . I had been examined and treated by 23 doctors till he got a hold of me.

. . . I too have been a victim of labyrinthitis—besides Drammamine, I was given nicotinic acid and I had to get new glasses.

. . . After trying several different kinds of medication, my doctor finally gave me a series of histamine injections and if I begin to hear a ringing I chew gum vigorously.

. . . I am happy to say I was cured by a radical mastoidectomy on my left ear.

. . . I believe we can treat the Eternal Ear with cold light crystals —like in the lightning bugs tail. I am a Rock Hound and believe in crystals.

. . . I am concerned about your health—the photo of you looks as if your hair is getting thin. I read that this is from a nervous condition.

. . . For medication I take Sansert. You might ask your doctor about this. I have found that 12–14 hours of *sound sleep* is a *great healer*. Ice packs relieve the pressure and you must remember that nature is a *great healer*.

. . . My difficulty, too, is Meniere's Disease—no one can ever know the suffering we have gone through unless they experience it. My physician gave me everything without favorable results. Someone told me to take Ascorbic Acid (Vit. C) 100 milligrams, after each meal and at bedtime—for a week—then increase each dose one tablet. When all symptoms left me I was taking 10 tablets.

. . . I'm writing to give you a little hint of something that I did which helped greatly. Whenever I even so much as turned over, started to sit up and tried to stand I fixed my eyes on the upper corner of the room where the walls & ceiling meet. I never *never* let them wander from that spot until I had turned or moved. Do not laugh at this or let your doctors scoff. My doctor was proud of me for figuring this out and told other patients about it.

. . . Remember Time heals everything—even labyrinthitis—P.S. a suggestion for your moments of dizziness—Hold your breath till it subsides.

. . . I have had recurring attacks of labyrinthitis for 25 years—I finally found a good doctor who prescribed Vit. B-12, one 25 MCG tablet daily—my dizziness cleared up immediately.

. . . Whatever lies ahead of you, if removal of the inner ear is considered do not wait until it is too late. During my operation the facial nerve was cut for it comes out at one of 8 different places behind the ear. My one ear is sharper now than my 2 together were. To safeguard the remaining ear you should have the adenoids removed to prevent future infection.

. . . Anyway, I am going to try to describe in a crude way the treatment I got. Metal pieces were put behind each ear and some kind of electric machine that looked like a big T.V. was attached. These electric waves that went through my head started me on the road to recovery. I hope you will plan to live in a warm, dry climate.

. . . Now and then I put a few drops hydrogen peroxide in my ears.

189

. . . eliminate the salt in your diet—completely.

. . . Please purchase a copy of "I believe in Miracles" by Katherine Kuhlman . . . You may want to fly to Pittsburgh to visit one of her meetings.

. . . I had this thing 32 years ago—when I fell in the shower. I was to take 4 rounded tablespoonsful of Epsom Salts in a full glass of water. *NO* other liquids for 24 hours. My first thoughts were—it would have a severe laxative action. The Dr. assured me to the contrary. My dizziness was gone following that period of time—the heavy salt solution acted as a dehydrant—draining the system of all fluids during that time . . .

. . . Don't take a drug called librium—I got dizzy from taking it.

. . . The clinic here has been able to do nothing for me. So, fella, if you are cured, how about letting me have the recipe?

. . . drink about 6 oz. of Hawaiian Pineapple juice every hour or hour & ½. It's supposed to stimulate the posterin part of the pituitary gland and that increases the excretion of urine. You will spend a lot of time in the bathroom but that should not hurt unless you have kidney trouble.

Some of the more lengthy medical advice follows:

From an Ex-Air Force Man
with a Machine That Might Be Helpful to Some People

I have heard about your affliction, and read about it. I am a victim of multiple sclerosis, which affects the nervous system. I have a visual handicap and lack of balance. I fell and broke my arm in January, due to the stability handicap. I am 46 years old and have three children. I went to a neurologist at the Cleveland Clinic who analyzed my illness. Our afflictions might be similar, in a way.

My youngest boy received a gyro for Christmas, which was about ten inches across, and which you cranked up. When holding it, I could feel the pull of the gyro, and it started me thinking it would help my stability. The doctor at the Clinic said it would not help me, because I am not able to correct fast enough when I feel myself off balance, but that there are a lot of diseases, even blindness, which it might help. I obtained a glider pilot turn-and-bank instrument, battery powered (a gyro). This one is about six inches square, but you probably would know in what sizes these can be made—the smaller the better I would say. You certainly have the best medical care available, so you possibly would be in a position to do something I've tried to do but can't get done. I am not physically able to

191

do it myself, and can't find the engineers, doctors, and technicians it takes to do it.

My idea from this turn-and-bank instrument is to strap it on your hip (with possibly a shoulder strap), one gyro up another one straight, and then bring the sound (the pitch) up to your ears, which would tell you if you're leaning forward it is off center. If you lean forward, you could possibly throw out the first 10 or 20 degrees of pitch, because when you take a step you actually throw it off, so you wouldn't want to hear the first 10 or 20 degrees off center, but if you make a turn over that you get a certain pitch in your ear; and if you are leaning forward or backward you get a little different pitch. The average person could then correct his balance, but with this M.S. it isn't possible to correct; it is a deterioration of the insulation of the nerves and maybe my balance center is all right, but maybe I'll send a message to my leg to go forward and it won't do it; it is liable to go backwards; the nerves could cross or something. I don't understand it; it is quite complicated. From what I have heard about your illness, it could be very similar up to a point—you can correct.

This gyro could do a lot of good for a lot of people, which is a lot of fun in life, doing something for somebody else. You might get a big bang out of doing something like this. You probably know what size gyros can be made, and you certainly can get hold of a neurologist—they're probably watching you like a hawk. If your handicap clears up—swell—I sure hope it does. But if it does or doesn't, you could possibly help somebody else, which you will find is probably more fun than orbiting the world.

From a Priest in Chicago

Just a note about dizziness. Almost a year ago I fell and shortly afterward got dizzy in spells. I have found that cold showers which cause me to take sharp deep breaths help me. Of course, you have the best doctors, but thought this might be a possibility. Best of luck.

ASK COL. WILLIAM J. DARROUGH, U.S. 21202
ASK MILTON SCHWABER, BALTO., MD. 21217
AND OTHERS

Can Ward Off As (The Fountain Of Youth) Well As Cure Sundry Ailments Not Caused By Germs. Polio. Paralysis. Heart Attacks Erysipelas. Heals Broken Bones. Incisions. Etcetera.

OVER

OVER   Ask Your Physician.

DIET RECIPE FOR CURING HEART AILMENTS, HEALING WOUNDS AND OTHER AILMENTS DUE TO IMPROPER FUNCTIONING OF THE CAPILLARY TUBES WHICH NOURISH EVERYTHING IN THE ANIMAL AND HUMAN ANATOMY.

My Legacy To The World.

Put one teaspoon of pure animal crystal Gelatine in a half pint china cup. Add three or four teaspoons of cold water and stir. Fill cup with boiling water and stir. As soon as it will not burn mouth, have afflicted person drink it hot, at least fifteen minutes before breakfast, once each week.

ALBERT ROSENBERG OF MICHAEL   BALTIMORE 17, MARYLAND   THE UNITED STATES OF AMERICA
Buy Only Unflavored Gelatine Sold In Grocery Stores.

ASK FORMER MAYOR, THOMAS D'ALESANDRO
H. COURTENAY JENIFER, TOWSON 4.

From a Woman in San Antonio, Texas

There is a very simple cure for dizziness! It came out about five years ago in a best selling book called "Folk Medicine of Vermont" by one Dr. Jarvis.
Here is the remedy: Try three cups a day.

VINEGAR TEA

One teaspoon APPLE CIDER VINEGAR
One teaspoon HONEY
Mix with one cup of warm water. Stir well
Sip slowly

The book said that very stubborn cases take three weeks, but every known cure I have heard of takes three days. I was cured of 15 years of dizziness in three days. Other cases I have heard of are similar.
It is absolutely harmless and almost free so give it a try. You can't lose. The dizziness never returns.

From a Woman in Swarthmore, Pennsylvania

It is a rainy afternoon, here in Swarthmore, Pennsylvania, and I am sitting at the typewriter, hoping it, (the typewriter) the room, and I will stay in focus and in one place until I finish this letter. I am a co-victim, along with you and how many others of this crazy ailment, labyrinthitis. If it wasn't so frustrating, angering, and depressing, I really should laugh. Here am I who has never been west of Pittsburgh, and you who have literally been out of this world, felled by the same strange malady. It's really very much like politics—you never know who you'll meet.

Anyway, every once in a while, when I get tired of explaining how I feel, and why I feel, etc., etc., to all those nice, well-meaning people who are always asking the same questions, I think how good it would be to just sit and talk to someone who would understand all the questions before they were even asked, mainly someone who suffers from the same complaints. So this is why I was thinking about you, and decided to write a letter since we're hardly next-door neighbors.

I suppose the doctors have you on these little blue and white silver-like pills of Anti-Vert which I'm convinced do nothing except transport me into some sort of twilight zone and leave me there drifting about in a phantomlike existence. I tried giving them up for a week but finally decided to go back to them; I'd rather drift than lurch. And besides it's more graceful. This is all the medication my poor doctor can offer me, except courage, patience, determination, and laughter, none of which however are available in our local drug store.

Don't you find that there are days when you wish you could very carefully lift your head right off your body, and walk away, leaving it with the newspapers, for the trashman to collect. It's inconceivable to me that six tiny, tiny semicircular canals can do to my head what they very thoroughly are managing to do. I'm sure you can appreciate the world of delicate mechanisms far better than I. But why can't they control these sensitive organs?

Have you discovered any new ways to live with this thing, other than those I guess we all acquire from just living with the situation —like moving totally, as if one were in a full-length cast, and stepping carefully and deliberately, as if one were walking on an earth made of egg shells. Maybe if we all pooled our knowledge, reactions, and experiments with this condition, one of us could come up with the right answer. Labyrinthitis must be just as unnerving to a Russian cosmonaut as to a Swarthmore housewife. Just better known.

Maybe by the time this crazy epistle reaches you, there will have been a sudden moment of absolute magic, and we both will be standing straight and secure again. I hope you have not felt I was presumptuous in writing. I feel better for having shared a rainy afternoon.

From a Doctor in Carthage, Tennessee

Thank you for your letter. I did not expect you to have time to answer.

I wish to add something to what I wrote you in the way of remedies.

I know you have all of the best medical care, but I have a special, I believe original method of using the usual nicotinic acid tablets that make your face flush for a few minutes, giving you freer circulation through the head. It is a wonderful treatment and usually gives very prompt and lasting results.

I submit this for your doctors' consideration.

The nicotinic acid in tablets are used by doctors generally, especially for dizziness.

It is commonly prescribed to be taken before each meal. Since the body becomes accustomed to it, and the face stops flushing, often, after the first day.

The flushing effect is necessary for benefit, so most of the benefit is lost after the first day, if it is taken in the ordinary pattern.

I have found that by taking two hundred milligram tablets, on rising, only a half hour before any food or drink, once or twice a week, the flush is always good.

No prescription is necessary. By this you may avoid surgery. Best wishes.

From a Doctor in Chicago

After reading the enclosed article, it seems as though you are a victim of Meniere's syndrome. Having been a victim of this myself and having treated it over the past few years, I have become very pragmatic. If the treatment works, I use it and there are many crutches to be used with Meniere's syndrome.

The thing that seems to cause the most trouble is movement of the head and my own experience shows the greatest crutch to these acute attacks of vertigo is making the head stationary and resistent to motion. I find that the easiest way to do this is by using a Thomas cervical collar. Many of the patients being treated by me for Meniere's syndrome are wearing this collar and having considerable relief and it has, in all cases, reduced the attacks of vertigo.

From a Man in Northbrook, Illinois

May I please suggest something that may ease your system.
I used it for a week when I had the flue with a little paddy—imported fine barley flavored whiskey.

From an Eye-Reader in Brooklyn, New York

You are in your helmet and uniform of an astronaut on the picture of the title page of Life of Feb. 2, 1962. Your photograph is very clear and distinct. I have never seen any eyes as well photographed as yours. I am in sympathy with you and I admire you who are an American national hero, therefore I wish to acquaint you with that what I read in your eyes.

I possess the art of reading in the eyes various diseases of human body. I read in your eyes on the picture that your bladder tends to have stones. I see in your eyes that you have at present a few stones in your bladder. You should consult a doctor, an urologist if possible. Only a careful examination by X-rays can determine the exact condition of your bladder.

From a Woman in New York City

When you recover I wish you could be sent by the gov't on a 50 state lecture tour at High Schools and *also* to parents *only* meetings.

The US-ers won't forget your quick, firm handling of those beer cans on a church lawn. It is this sort of talk you should give American kids & parents.

I do so feel for you & your wife during this trying period & lost desires but you'll make the U. S. Senate for we need you—even as a President some day! (Yes!!)

I wish you would buy one of those $25.00 electric juicers. Drinking chlorophyll drinks will help your body correct things & heal.

Every day I drink the juice & all of a handful of *green* leaves (chard, dandelion greens, etc.)

Get well & good luck!

From a Twenty-Nine-Year-Old
Woman in Ft. Worth, Texas

If I may, I'd like to add another discovery of interest I have come across since all this happened to me. I have found out that the nerves of the body end in the hands and feet. They are strongest in the feet and if these endings are massaged it will stimulate blood to that organ to which the nerve goes. Actually, the nerve ending hurts when that organ which it feeds is in need of stimulas. If you are not familiar with this, try it. It really works. Get someone to massage your toes (or do it yourself if you can do it comfortably) and soles with a knuckle and/or fingers and find out where things hurt. For instance tired or strained eyes will show up on the "eye toe" or jangled nerves will show up in the vicinity for that.

Around the base of the big toe is where the inner ear is. Massage it a lot, for I'm sure you will find it very sensitive.

I have enclosed a diagram which I have haphazardly scraped together for your information. To the best of my knowledge all the markings are accurate. Do try it. See what you think.

Left

Right

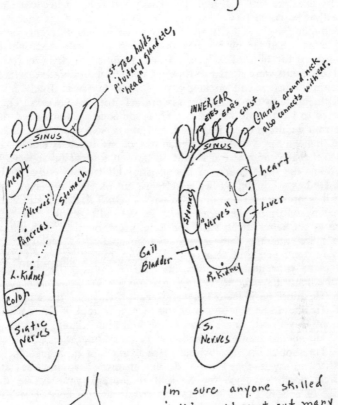

1st toe holds pituitary gland etc, "head"

INNER EAR
EYES EARS   chest
Glands around neck also connects with ear.

SINUS

SINUS

heart

heart

Stomach

Stomach

"Nerves"

"Nerves"

Pancreas.

Liver

Gall Bladder

L. Kidney

R. Kidney

Colon

Siatic Nerves

S. Nerves

thyroid gland

I'm sure anyone skilled
in this could point out many
more than this, but it is a start.
Massage the toes on <u>top</u> and in
<u>back</u> and <u>between</u> the toes.

From a Woman in McKeesport, Pennsylvania

To Mrs. John H. Glenn, Jr.

I have followed the newspaper reports on your husband's unfortunate accident. It is now eight weeks and by tonight's paper I see that his troubles are still with him. I feel very sad about it because I am sure that he could be helped were he to go to the right source.

Sometime ago I did damage to my spine in two different ways—one being a bad fall off a bench that tipped over. I landed right on the side of my head. The reason I am prompted to write to you is that the results were similar to those of your husband's fall: dizziness, vomiting, nausea, and an inability to move my head freely.

I put up with the pains and discomforts for three weeks. There seemed to be no help for me, so when someone recommended that I consult a chiropractor, I listened, and put myself under Dr ———— care. Believe me, I thank God each day of my life that I did so.

I feel that your husband would do himself a great favor were he to follow the same course of action since his trouble is due to his fall. He has no doubt, pushed a vertebra out of place in such a way that it is pressing on one or more nerves. Until that pressure is relieved by returning the vertebrae to its natural position, he cannot hope to get better. If he waits too long, a pathological change may take place, and the damage may not be able to be repaired.

Why don't you find some capable chiropractor in your vicinity and place your husband under his care. I consider the following requirements important:

1. He must be able to take and read X-Rays of the spine.
2. He should be a graduate of the Palmer School of Chiropractic of Davenport, Iowa. (This is the first and original school).
3. He should use a neurocalometer. (very important)
4. He should use the "whole in one" method of adjusting.

All I can say is—that I would do this at once. I wouldn't ask any medical doctor's advice for he will discourage your taking this course of action. I shall be thankful myself all the days of my life that I acted and acted quickly.

Through television and newspapers I know your husband is a fine young man. Our country needs men of his calibre, so I'd be very glad to see him well and happy again, to be of service to his family, community, and country.

The sad expression on his face in the newspaper pictures haunts me. I just had to write to you to suggest a course of action I know will be helpful. Please don't delay.

200

From an Ex-Marine

Dear Semper Fidelis:

You must have the softest noggin in the history of the Marines. I have seen Marine heads hit with Wisky and beer bottles, rifle butts, chairs, tables, 155's, grenades, "rolling pins" etc. and it made no impression, never mind depressions.

I am your Amigo, not only because of the "Halls Montezuma" but I am of the opinion with you on the ticket President Johnson will carry Ohio.

With Steve Young he will get beat by 250,000 votes. Get off your "Duff" and "Move Marine." May I respectfully suggest "get-out" "Vamuse" into a Naval Hospital and you will recover *Pronto*.

God Bless you and *you pray* for all the Marine dead that made you and I proud to be a Leatherneck.

Glenn: I have solved your problem. Those Methodist Milkshakes ruined you. Start drinking Wisky that all Marines do.

From a Man in Marion, Ohio

While playing golf one day I stooped over and was later told by a doctor that I had given myself a "mild treatment." If I understand your case correctly, you have contracted vertigo which is a form of the affliction of the inner ear, which I presume you have. At least this is what it says in the newspapers, and I am telling you how I treated myself which is as follows.

I laid over the bed with my head on the floor and counted to one hundred. I have cured myself at least three time of this inner ear trouble.

If you wish to try this treatment, all power to you because I know it works.

From a Lumberman in Torrington, Connecticut

If, by adding a couple of spoonsful of honey to your daily diet, your condition should improve to some degree, it might be our Father's way of telling us, through you, that there are many very important things to learn, here on Earth, before we should venture into the Heavens.

From a Woman in Sheboygan, Wisconsin

I felt so bad for you when I read in the paper about your illness. I have very much sympathy for you, because I have the same condition.

I was 18 years old when I first got the first attack. I can remember I was working one day feeling fine and long about noontime I became very dizzy and I thought at the time the whole world was on a merry go around and I couldn't walk without falling down, and became very sick to my stomach, and I can remember the only thing I could do was go to bed, and lie very still. It seemed like I couldn't even bear have anybody as much as walk accross the room because the least little vibration would arouse me and make me start to nauseate again.

I don't know how many doctors I went to see before they finally found out what it was and believe me I felt like I just wanted to die. When they finally found out they called it a severe case of Meniere's disease and its an inflammation of the middle ear, so when I read in the paper that you had this, I began to cry because I know exactly how you feel, and what you are going thru. I wouldn't wish this condition on my worse enemy because its a very very mean thing to have and that why I felt so bad for you.

Maybe I shouldn't of written to you this letter, because I don't in any way want to discourage you, but the reason I did write is I want you to have patience with yourself the condition will leave you, it will maybe take a few years, but it will go away. It had it so bad that several times I wanted to end my life, but I kept saying to myself. You're going to get better. Don't lose confidence. I get shots from the doctors yet and I am now 46 years old, and frankly right now I feel wonderful. I never have to go to bed no more for this and I am very thankful to the Dear Lord, because he did help me.

Sometimes hearing from other people and knowing the wonderful results they received with the same condition can inspire you and I know at the time if someone would of have written to me telling me this I would have ran to them right away and I would of done anything just to know anything about it, so Mr. Glenn don't be mad at me for writing to you. I want to help you because I felt real bad for you. You're a wonderful man from what I know and seen you do on television. What wonders you did for our country and I am going to pray real hard for you so you will recuperate rapidly because people like you we need badly.

If ever you want to write to me and want to know anything more about this condition I will be more than happy to tell you, but do keep your chin up you are going to feel swell again someday. No fooling.

P.S. If ever you are in Sheboygan and you want to talk to me about this I will be more than happy to help you. I also don't think you got this from your fall in the bathroom either, I didn't fall and I had it bad and I don't know where mine came from. I'm not trying to dispute the doctors but sometimes these things can come from nowhere.

From an Ex-Marine in Chicago

Dear Sir: As a former Marine (Paris Island 1917) I feel it is my duty to tell you of my experience of "dizziness."

When I joined the Marine Corps I had perfect equilibrium and had no alergies. After the war I was discharged from the Corps and I joined the Army of Occupation. In 1922 in a scrub game of baseball I got hit on the top of the forehead with a line drive. I recovered o.k.

Then about 1940 my wife got some, what I thought at the time, was some spoiled chicken. After eating it I got violently dizzy right in bed. I thought I would fall off the bed at the time. I didn't go to the doctor but as my dizziness continued less violent I gradually discovered that I was alergic to chicken, and any slight touch of egg even. I can't eat anything with eggs in it, or I get dizzy again.

I stopped eating fowl and egg in any form and felt much better.

Then I got an ear infection following a cold and my ear drum burst. Sheer coincidence. Lo and behold after my doctor gave me a couple of shots of penicillin both the ear ache and all dizziness left me—But here is what I want to tell you—I presume your doctors know about it—but just in case they don't—Shortly after my ear incident I read Doctor Bundensen who was Health Commissioner of Chicago . . . He told about a condition in the ear that makes people violently dizzy at times. And that the only way to cure the dizziness is to perforate the ear drum. So that's it. When I heard of your withdrawal, I knew you are pretty sick. Ask your doctor if stopping eating eggs or puncturing your eardrum would help.

From a Man in Escondido, California

When I was in college I was out for track and during the winter we took build up exercises in the gym because it was too cold and blustery outside to run. One day I wrenched my back and the next day we had to do double time outside for the ROTC training. Ordinarily a little double time jog would have been easy for me, but this time I could not do it at all. I got the most awful pain on my left side. I thought I was developing heart trouble. They took me to the hospital and taped me up with those wide strips of adhesive tape —said I had pleurisy. After a couple of weeks when I had gotten no better and was complaining to my roommate how my side still hurt, he looked up from his lessons and said, "I'll bet you have a rib out of place. Why don't you go to an osteopath?"

The next day I did. He put me on his table, ran his fingers up and down my back and stopped just below my shoulder blades on the left side. He said, "You have got a rib out of place". He worked me over a bit and then pressed heavily at that point and I heard a snap. He heard it too and said, "Now get up and take a deep breath". Well, after about three weeks I was almost afraid to take a deep breath, but I did, slowly, and no pain. The next day I felt real good, but, stupid like I got to wrestling that evening and snapped it out again and the pain came back. Back to the osteopath and he put it back in place. Altogether it took about a month before the osteopath got it so it would stay in.

Since that time the osteopaths have developed a bone adjustment for the bones of the head, skull and cranium for people who have been bumped on the head or otherwise twisted their head in some way. I don't know much about it except that it works and the adjustments don't hurt. It has to do with restoring the normal movements of the bone segments with the sutures that occur about twelve times a minute. When these are right everything else is OK.

From a Man in San Francisco

I feel that I have know you all my life, so I'm taking the liberty to write to you about your sickness.

I too suffered the very same sickness as stated in the papers. I know what your going through. I belong to the Kaiser Plan here in San Francisco Bay area and they gave me a going over for about 4 months and finally told me I had to live with it. The first thing I done was stop taking the pills and took whiskey instead and stayed in bed for 3 or 4 days. The pills made me very nervous. When I got these spells my mind played tricks with me. I felt I was going to be a cripple the rest of my life and I was at the end of the line, I was ready to throw in the towel and call it quits. I was 42 years old then and I am 49 now and in pretty good shape tho I stagger now and then when I am walking. I take a couple of shots of whiskey before dinner that helps quiet my nerves after a hard day at work. You can do the same.

There's a movement to draft you. Anyway let your backer's go ahead it will be about that time when you will be ready to get in the race with good health.

So chin up fellow and don't give up there's plenty of everything in life ahead for you and for your lovely family.

From a Woman in Los Angeles

It nearly broke my heart to see you laid up when you were talking with Walter Cronkite tonight on T.V. You see after your trip into the "blue yonder" we all feel that you belong to us all.

The reason for this letter is that I had practically the same thing happen to me that happened to you. The only difference is and was that I slipped on an icy street and hit my head on the curbing.

I spent thousands of dollars on doctor bills trying to find out why the dizziness. One doctor tried one grain of thyroid and it worked. Before I started taking the thyroid every morning I was an absinthe drunk, staggering and falling.

The X-rays showed that before I took thyroid the large gland that goes back of the inner-ear and down the neck was swollen and pressed on the inner-ear. After taking the thyroid (even tho I was not deficient in thyroid) the gland shrank and the pressure was removed so the dizziness disappeared. Taking one thyroid pill each morning is very simple and I am fine and enjoy life.

Please ask your doctors to try it for just three days. One grain cannot hurt you and might help. If it does not work for you as it did for me I am sorry.

STARS IN THEIR EYES

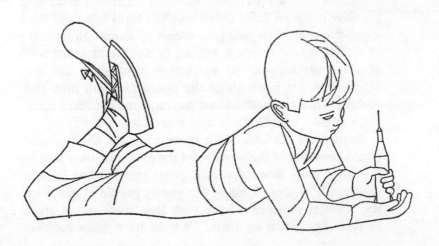

CHAPTER 14

Letters from the younger generation are always interesting for they bring an uninhibited candor, frankness, and fresh viewpoint that often puts their elders to shame. In fact, one of the impressive things in talking or writing to young folks of about the ten-year-old age group or older, is that they often know far more about the space program than their parents. This is something that has happened in "their time," not way back with Dad's "—now when I was a boy."

Beyond the confines of the space program, their perspective, knowledge of the world, and the events that are shaping it are far more developed at a given age than we knew as children. The more I see of the young people in this country, the less patience I have with the "professional crepehangers and doom-mongers." We do have great problems facing us now and in the future, but we have an even greater gang of young folks now developing to cope with those problems. The future looks good with them coming along to backstop us.

But this is not an essay, so let's enjoy the following excerpts.

From a Seventh-Grade Boy in Georgia

I watched you last year, when you went in to space. You were really great! You top Thomas Jefferson in my book (and that's pretty high because I am from Virginia.

I am in 7th grade an we are having an S.A. contest. I don't know who to write about, you or Thomas Jefferson. You see, we have to write about a patriot. If you would write a statement on what you think a great patroit is I might have a chance in the contest.

From a Girl in Pennsylvania

I'm a senior in high school and a college-bound student. As an American teenager, looking hopefully toward our country's future and feel that all teenagers experienced today the same desperate desire for your safety and the accomplishment of your mission. I can best illustrate this with a brief description of the crowded, darkened room where many of us watched Friendship 7 take off. As the lucky students who had begged their way out of classes piled most noisily into the room, they slowly became aware of the tenseness transmitted even to us over the television. The count-

down, nearing its last few minutes, produced an extreme hush. A short hold caused a spontaneous moan of disappointment. After resuming, the final seconds slipped by in a painful quiet. Many of us found it difficult to control the tears and earnest prayers we held for you and, more selfishly, for our future also. During the first minutes of your flight, the utter silence reflected our hopes, and thoughts of you followed us all during the day.

I cannot say how I feel. Relief and joyous admiration flood my heart.

From a Girl in Canton, Ohio

I congratulate you on your flight. I do wish, very much that I could meet you. I sort of did meet you, in a dream. We . . . by we I mean you and I. Well, we both were going up in the "Friendship 7" together. You had a regular spacesuiet on but mine had a little silver scurt on it. My foot was just in the capsule when my mother called me to watch you on T.V.

If I could pick a father from the whole world, I would pick you. You see, I don't have a father, he died when I was 5 months old, he stept on a mine . . .

Would you give me, please an autograph of your self. So I could at least look at your face.

I am not as godly as you are. But I must tell you that I prayed to God and asked him to let you live three times. I almost started to cry when they couldn't find you.

From a Young Texan

John would you know if you were going to land in Texas next or not? I live in Wichita Falls, Texas. That is why I ask.

210

Mrs. Warren Sinsheimer
22 Murray Hill Road
Scarsdale, New York

Dear Colonel Glenn,

I think you are wonderful for going to space. Can you come to my house for dinner next Fri?

LOVE
Alan, 6 yrs.

From a Blind Girl in Massachusetts

I have written you before, but I thought maybe my letter got lost in the mail. Boy, I bet you must have a billion letters to answer. You should get a typest for you.

One night I had the sisiest dream. I dreamed that you came here and I met you. Of course, I know that that couldn't come true. In the first place you are too buisy. I hope some day I can meet you and Mrs. Glenn and Lynn and David. I have written to Mrs. Glenn, Lynn, and David once. Now I'm writting to you twice.

Today, we surprised my braille teacher. We had just come back from chorus and she wasn't in the room. We decided to get in line without her help. When she came in, she said that she was proud of us. So, she didn't give us any homework. Usually, we have to wright something in the news. Most of the time before you went into orbit, I wrote about you. You are my favorite subject. In school when we were discussing your space shot, I had my hand up for a lot of questions.

I don't go to a blind school . . . There are only six blind children. The rest can see. It is a public school. When I explained it to some of my friends in North Reading, they ask, "Are the rest cripple or something?" Well, they aren't . . .

From a Teenage Boy in New York

In you, Colonel Glenn, and in your family, as in the other astronauts and their families, are found all the ideas and ideals of Americana. You hold a valuable lesson for all, especially the young Americans, nay all the young citizens of the world. All of you stand for all that is right, from the four basic freedoms of a democracy, to those basic laws of morality which ought to govern everyone's life. We need more like you!

From a Boy in Cincinnati, Ohio

I watched the space show. It was O.K. except for the end. I stayed up all morning wondering when you may go into space. Even if I wanted to watch something else, I couldn't. The space show was on every station.

From a Girl in Armonk, New York

When you were in the parde we made ticker tape and we threw it at the t.v.

From an Eleven-Year-Old New Hampshire Girl

The day you went up into space my dog Lassie have nine puppy. So we are going to name one John Glenn.

From Two Girls, Members of a
Florida High-School Choral Group

We felt that even though we as teenagers could not give you any physical assistance, we wanted to help you in some other way.
At approximately ten minutes before the actual take-off, we realized that we were all silently praying. We stood, bowed our heads,

213

and reverently sang "The Lord Bless You", dedicating it to you because we felt the words and meaning expressed our heartfelt thoughts.

We would like people to know that contrary to many ideas adults have, we teenagers have some feeling about important world affairs and the people involved in them.

From a Twelve-Year-Old New Hampshire Boy

That was some shot. I watched every minute of it (postponements and all) and I thought it was neat. Although when the heat shield was reported loose I really started to worry.

They sure can pack enough equipment into one capsule that size and still have room for you. If they made cars that way pedestrians would have to be careful not to step on them.

From a Fifth-Grader in Fort Lauderdale, Florida

I knew you would go around yesterday because I prayed that you would. (Yesterday was my lucky day too because I hit my first home run.) All the people will remember you for a little while and then people will forget about you but I will never forget you.

From a Young Hoosier

I am in the forth grade and I watched your flight through space. I wish I was with you and some times my mother wishes I was too.

From a Young Boy in Oklahoma

Bert Buffington and I are building a rocket and we would like to have some blueprints of the Atlas. Could we have blueprints of what is in the capsule and of what is in the boster? Could we have the ingredients that you put in the RP-1 and liquid oxygen . . .

From Two Third-Grade Boys in Ohio

John Glenns family did't wiggle a round to nuch and his wife kiss Him on the cheek and was proud of Him.

Letter in Braille from a Blind
Fourth-Grade Girl in Kansas

I wonder what it looks like up in the rocket. Do you know how long it takes to orbit around the earth three times?

I heard a man on the radio say "I don't know if you can hear me or not," when you just started flight.

215

How does it feel to be up in space? I'd like to go up there someday.

Do you like waiting day after day before you get a chance to go up in space?

I have had an experience I will never forget but it doesn't seem as interesting as going up in space.

From a Third-Grade Boy in Ohio

Col. John Glenn didn't act silly when the President congratalate him. And his family didn't act silly when they standed up. He said that he didn't want all the credit. And always John Glenn would say we. He wouldn't of made this flight if it wasn't for the other men.

From a Boy in Flushing, New York

If I could go on your next trip I have to know soon and in enough time to tell Sister St. Augustus that I will be absent from school. Then the whole class will pray for us. I am 7 years old and in good health.

From an Eight-Year-Old Virginia Boy

I think they can make a rocket that can go to the moon. How would you like to come and see my pet boa constrictor?

216

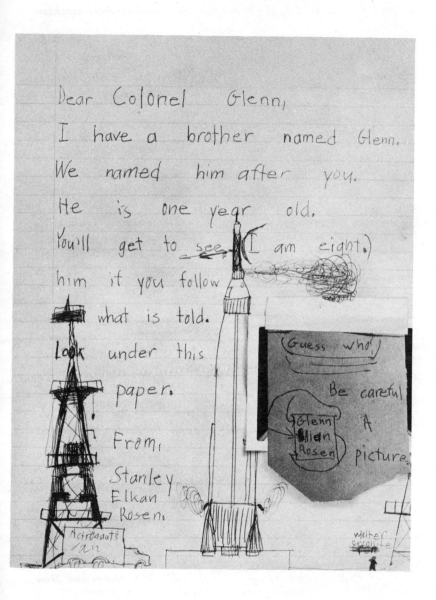

Dear Colonel Glenn,
I have a brother named Glenn.
We named him after you.
He is one year old.
You'll get to see (I am eight.)
him if you follow
what is told.
Look under this
paper.

From,
Stanley
Elkan
Rosen.

Guess who?

Be careful
A
picture.

Glenn
Alan
Rosen

Astronauts
van

walter
erquite

217

Dear Colonel Glenn.
Here is mrs. Glenn
doing the twist.
We love her.
We love You.

Mrs.
Glenn.

From an Eighth-Grade Boy in Fair Lawn, New Jersey

A friend of mine has a theory on what the shiny particles outside of your capsule were. Probably no one will believe it, but it might be true. Those particles could be some kind of communication from an alien world. They might reveal to another planet how far advanced our world is in space technology. Could it be possible?

From a Ten-Year-Old Girl in Omaha, Nebraska

I am ten years old. I think you are the most wonderful man in the world. I said prayers for you all day long. We couldn't watch tee vee but we listened to the radio. In the afternoon we got to watch tee vee. I am sure underneath you were a little scared. I would have been, too. Your name was put down in my diary. You will always be down in my mind.

From a Girl in Jacksonville, Florida

I'm so thankful to God that you made it safely! I am proud to be an American with such wonderful atvantages, which are better than Russian children . . .
. . . Mom was so happy she started to cry!

219

From a Girl in Ithaca, Illinois

I was so happy when they said you were all right. I had to cross my fingers so I wouldn't faint.

About two days after the flight, I made a paper bag space suit, with a foil mirror, a paper bag mask, a toy speaker, and a air condition.

Say, I've been talking to you so much I think it is time to leave now!

From an Oklahoma Girl

I want to congratulate you on your terrific space flight. We watched you on T.V. at school. I'm sure glad you went up on a week day instid of a week end because all we did all day was watch you on T.V.

From a Nine-Year-Old Girl in Webster, Texas

I am sorry you bumped your head. I hope you fill better. I am the sister of the boy who said, "If I was twenty one I'd vote for you."

From Another Texas Girl

I am sorry you hurt your head. I'm the girls friend of the girls brother that said if he were 21 he would vote for you.

From a Fifth-Grade Class in Rico Riviera, California

To celebrate your great achievement we were all served cake for lunch today. We'd like for you to go again!

9 Roseld Court
Deal, New Jersey
Feb 21, 1962

Dear Colonel Glenn,

I guess you were scared when the rocket blasted off. For such an event, I would wear my yellow-flower dress. Did you feel funny when you knew everyone in the world was watching you on television? I hope you'll like to know I watched you on T.V. If I saw the world from such a place, I would feel extremely odd. But I don't know too much about flying around in a rocket. With a steak for breakfast, I don't know at all how one could be nervous. Would you please send me an autograph? My family would be very happy.

Sincerely Yours,
Wendy Kaufman

From an Eleven-Year-Old Boy in Paris, Illinois

I was sorry you got ready 10 times and got postponed 10 times. You be sure and tell Alan Shepard, Gus Grissom and D. Slate hello Col. I want a special hello to Mrs. Glenn Jr. and Sr. Lyn is my favorite of the Glenn family. Tell David he has a nice personality, reminds me of cousin Jerry in Indiana.

From a Boy in Anaheim, California

My name is Bradley and I am seven years old and in the 2nd grade. I Have a question to ask you. I asked my mother and father and some other people but they don't know. If God created the world, who created God? The Bible says that God created the Heaven and the Earth, but it doesn't say where God was before he did this. Do you think he created another planet where people are living?

From an American Girl in
Ludwigsburg, West Germany

We are all happy you are alive. My whole family was stuck to the radio, and even at supper they were still listening . . .
While we were listening when you were coming down, my little brother, Jimmy, was scared and thought you were going to get him.

222

From a Sixth-Grade Girl in New York

We watched your flight into orbit. Your full of good luck. The other sixth grade watched TV with us and I met a boy and now were going steady.

From a Lad in Daly City, California

In our class we listened on the raido to your flight It was very seccesfully. We were very happy I felt like it was a mew world I was very happy. We are still talking about it. I know you felt, you must have been scared. We heard when you passed Astralia they all turned on there lights that must have been exciting. Could you *please* tell us how you felt. We are all very excited. Roses are red/vetols are blue/when you went around the wrold/we did to. We are thankful for all the sinestists who made the flight secesfully.

From a Young Girl in Hazlet, New Jersey

Congratulation on your flight.
The day you were shot I watched you go up on T.V. in school.
What was it like up there?
I would like to have a picture and your autograph. If you have an extra stamp will you send me one. I will enclose 5 cents.

P.S. "ABOUT
THAT CRATE OF EGGS..."

CHAPTER 15

Maybe we can drop the letter opener for awhile. Hope you've enjoyed this small session.

Oh, yes,—as to that crate of fresh eggs. I knew we couldn't possibly use them all, so I called our pastor, Rev. Frank Erwin, for a little unusual ministerial guidance. As usual, Frank rose to the occasion and away went the eggs to a downtown mission.

We received a later report regarding the number of people the crate served at breakfast the next morning, but I can't locate that letter. If you come across it . . .

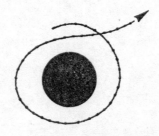

A WORD
FROM THE PUBLISHERS

(These letters praising John Glenn were independently compiled by the editors of World Book Encyclopedia Science Service, Inc.)

One of the functions of a hero is the reaffirmation of age-old values. Love of God, love of country, bravery, courage, dedication, humility—these words occur over and over again in the more than 175,000 letters written to Lt. Col. John H. Glenn, Jr. following his successful three-orbit flight of February 20, 1962.

If Glenn or any other man had suddenly become the first American to orbit the Earth, the bare deed itself would have made him a kind of spontaneous hero. But it is apparent from the reaction of his countrymen that John Glenn's mod-

est eloquence, his understated sense of humor, his una-
bashed religious faith, the unique stability of his personality
in the perilous presence of sudden fame created—almost instantly—a rare extra dimension that people everywhere were
hungry to embrace. The extremely trying role he naturally
assumed not only personified the deed, it also lifted him
head and shoulders above the synthetic heroes Americans
were accustomed to making of movie actors, TV cowboys,
and rock-and-roll singers.

Americans reacted to him as they had previously reacted
to another colonel who also often used the expression "we,"
Charles Lindbergh, and as they had reacted to the hero image
of Eisenhower, MacArthur, and Kennedy.

In fact, few if any combinations of deed and personality
since Lindbergh's historic 33-hour, 39-minute flight across
the Atlantic in 1927 have so captured the public imagination.

One purely statistical index is the amount of paper show-
ered on the streets of New York during a hero's welcome.
The Lindbergh parade resulted in 1,750 tons of paper. That
was topped by the deluge for General Douglas MacArthur
upon his return from command in the Far East—3,249 tons.
The John Glenn parade in New York, however, set a new,
all-time record as sanitation department workers hauled
away 3,474 tons of paper from the streets.

Another index is comments aroused in the nation's press.
The New York Times' Washington Bureau Chief, James Res-
ton—a man not noted for sentimentality—wrote: "The examples placed before a nation are vital. What we constantly
observe we tend to copy. What we admire and reward we
tend to perpetuate. This is why John Glenn himself is almost
as important as his flight into outer space, for he dramatizes
before the eyes of the whole nation the noblest qualities

of the human spirit . . . Is the moon worth John Glenn when we need him so badly on earth?"

Women, especially, reacted to both deed and the man with unashamed emotion. Columnist Dorothy Kilgallen wrote, "I am madly in love with him by special permission of my husband . . . For the first time in my life I sat glued to my TV set for hours, eating peanut butter sandwiches and crying."

Small town columnist Mary McCarthy of the Los Altos, California *Local Enterprise* wrote: "His great value is the shining example he gave to a whole nation: courage, dedication, humility and a sense of humor! What a wonderful four-pronged spading fork to dig up and revitalize the spiritual soil of this entire land."

But perhaps the most reliable index of all was furnished by the letter writers of grass-roots America who—by the tens of thousands—put pen to paper and told John Glenn what he personally meant to them and to America.

As the letters printed here demonstrate, it is interesting that the spontaneous reaction stemmed not so much from the deed as from the man whom millions saw on television as he translated a superb engineering feat into the human terms of a national aspiration.

The appeal, first of all, was what the research world of Madison Avenue calls "horizontal," that is, all age and income groups were represented—from first graders to men of forty, from teen-age girls to matrons, from religious crackpots to conscientious ministers, and from Park Avenue to R.F.D. No. 3 in Pineville, North Carolina.

He received, almost simultaneously, a gold star from a child in Coraopolis, Pennsylvania, and this testimony from a thirty-six-year-old woman in Middletown, Rhode Island:

"Lately, I realized my generation was doing something and was quite fit to do so . . . Now, instead of sitting around waiting for the bomb to drop, we are going to start doing things . . . We can do anything we set our minds to. We're young!"

People everywhere instinctively trusted John Glenn. "You might caution American youngsters on the importance of safe play," wrote an Indianapolis, Indiana, man. "They will listen to you."

"I felt so drawn to him," wrote an Apollo, Pennsylvania man to John Glenn's parents. "He seemed like my own son."

The parents of two girls in La Crosse, Washington, wrote Colonel Glenn, "Please forgive the American public for being a little silly and sentimental, but we needed a hero badly and you filled the bill far and above our wildest dreams."

In response, John Glenn tackled the herculean task of answering as many letters as he could. He was particularly attentive to letters from scout and school groups, from mothers and widows of Marines killed in action, from handicapped children and—stemming from his often-avowed Christian faith—from people interested in religion.

Americans by the hundreds wrote to ask him for his favorite music ("I like many selections; music is the language of the emotions"), his favorite poems ("Your teacher may not thank me for suggesting this but try reading *The Shooting of Dan McGrew*"); his favorite hymn (*Be Still My Soul*); and his favorite Bible verses (*Ecclesiastes 3:1–3* and *Psalm 139:9–10*).

They also wrote him about his opinion of right and wrong ("Right, as a Hemingway character once said, is what you feel good after."); his views on smoking ("It can apparently do no good and may do great harm—so why start?"); the relationship between science and religion ("Actually the more I learn in science the more I feel I am proving God's existence."); his favorite prayer ("God grant me the serenity to accept the things I cannot change, courage to change the

231

things I can, and the wisdom to know the difference.").

In answer to many inquiries as to whether he felt God was with him in his flight, he replied that he was rather busy in orbit but that "It should be a comforting thought to all of us that no matter where we go or what we do, we will never be alone."

One of his answers contained words he himself might well have recalled following his resignation from the nation's space program and the serious injury in Columbus, Ohio, that removed him from his candidacy for the U. S. Senate.

"We don't know all the answers in this life," he replied to a handicapped boy in Little Falls, New York. "And there comes a time when we must accept what happens and still not let it affect what we believe."

One thing is evident in the letters to and from the astronaut. John Glenn felt a personal responsibility to live up to and sustain the hero image his deed and personality had created. Living up to a nation's adopted symbol is never an easy task, for the greater the praise the greater the responsibility. Perhaps he realized this when he read the following bald praise from a woman in Canton, Ohio:

"John Glenn, you're a man's man, a child's hero and a mother's vision of her own son."

This quality of embodying the hopes, fears, and aspirations of a broad spectrum of the American people is eloquently illustrated in the letters of praise which follow.

To Annie Glenn from a Woman in Miami, Florida

I have never really prayed in my life before. I'm of the Catholic faith.

One and one half years ago, my husband left me. Three months later, I was in a severe automobile accident. First, I was not expected to live, but later they decided they might have to amputate both of my legs.

Today, my husband is back home, and I am walking.

When your husband, Mr. Glenn, took off into space, a tear came into my eyes, and I PRAYED FOR THE FIRST TIME. . . . . . . that he may come back alive.

It is true, in his interview when he said that God is not with us just for emergency, etc., but is always with us.

He has given to me once again, my belief and faith.

A Woman in Rochester, New York, Writes:

Thank you from the bottom of my heart for what you have done for America! How can I ever begin to put into words how I feel about you and all that you represent—its like trying to express how you feel about "Old Glory"—Valley Forge, Abraham Lincoln, the Fourth of July.

You have awakened the hearts and minds of all of us—to what America and the word "American" really stands for—Faith—Courage—Humility—Love of God and Country.

You possess all these qualities plus your own "inimitable smile and personality." And in all your appearances before the public, no matter where or what the circumstances your inate goodness and kindness—your courteous consideration and thoughtfulness of others showed in everything you did and said.

God Bless you and yours!

P.S. I've just got to add this—and I *mean* it in all seriousness and sincerity. PLEASE be our President some day!

From a Family in Purcellville, Virginia

An Astronaut and his wonderful family, who has kept an average, American, country family in complete uproar since February 20, 1962, 6:15 A.M. If you, Lt. Col. Glenn, will keep your feet on the ground now, we will be able to resume a normal way of living. We will eat regular, dry our eyes, accomplish the chores, stop running over each other running two television sets and a radio for news coverage, clipping newspapers and magazines for scrapbooks. Mom won't have to say, "Goodnight John", or, "Will you please go to bed, John, so this household will go to bed". (11:00 P.M. news, red-eyes, bug-eyed, STILL looking for news of John).

One thing we won't do and that is, stop talking. Lt. Col. John H. Glenn, Jr. is now a household word. "George", the parakeet, is in Orbit, with rigid training of trying to say— "As-tro-not-Glenn-a-o-k-go".

You all have our Best Wishes and Prayers, Always.

From "Just 6" of the happy million folks,

From a Couple in Van, Texas

We are so sorry about your accident but you will be fine I know. May God continue to bless you and everything you do.

To know we have men like you and families like yours to repre-sent America we are thankful. Young and old alike pray for you. You have given us so much courage, worthwhile ideals and deeper understanding these are what America needs. You are among our very greatest men.

We know your happiness comes from the heart. You, your wife and children are precious to us. Our prayers are yours. We have a son, wife and three fine grandchildren. Your standards are a pattern for all of us. Thank you for being just yourselves.

A Mother in Shelby, Ohio, Writes:

When some one does something nice for me or my family I al-way let them know how much it means to me.

You made my 5 year old son, Patrick, a very happy little boy when you had a member of your staff write him a letter. You are a *big* influence on Patrick and he tries to be very grown up.

I had to take him in to have some small blood vessels burned in-side his nose, due to frequent and heavy nose bleeds. He climbed on the table, closed his eye and let the doctor work away. He said, "John Glenn's buddies have to be brave!"

Patrick is cross-eyed and has worn heavy glasses for 1-½ years. Two months ago, the doctor said he had to wear a patch on his left eye at all times, until his right eye got stronger. This didn't slow our Patrick down. He said, "John Glenn has to stay in bed all the time, so I can wear my patch for awhile!"

Mr. Glenn, it seems as it you have helped this family over the worst ordeals! The morning you made your orbital flight, I was undergoing major surgery. As I was being wheeled to the operating room, I kept thinking, if you could do that alone, I could enter surgery alone! I just had to get out of the operating room alive and in one piece to watch T.V. and keep track of you! I didn't think much about the awful surgery I was to face because I was so interested in the big thing you were doing. The doctors told me later I was one of the most relaxed patients ever to enter the operating room. I told them I didn't have time to dwell on my troubles, I had to give my attention to John Glenn. I hope you don't mind the way we depend on you in our times of strife.

I heard today that you have withdrawn from the race. Not forever, I hope. This is just a slight delay! When you are well, you can pick up where you left off. I was forced to quit school in my eleventh year. I haven't given up hope of going back and finishing. I haven't given up, just got slightly delayed. Keep thinking that this is what happened to you. You can't give up now. You have 7 of our votes and with Patrick campaigning, who knows how far you can go.

Mr. Glenn, we continue to pray for you and again I thank you from the bottom of my heart for "just being the greatest thing to happen to our Patrick." May God bless you and keep you.

A Woman in Canoga Park, California, Writes:

As Alexander King said on the Jack Paar show last night, "the most wonderful thing about your flight is that one hundred and eighty million people in the United States, and people in other countries, forgot their individual creeds—their color and race and joined together in one great prayer for your safety and success."

We—in the United States, know there is tremendous P-O-W E-R in prayer.

Please remember to thank the people for their prayers.

From a Mother in Coraopolis, Pennsylvania

I am writing this for my four year old daughter, Jennifer Renee. On that exciting and prayerful Tuesday, the 20th of February, she was as emotionally attentive to the television as I was. She sat quietly and watched during the tense countdown and blast off.

When at last it was announced that you were "in orbit", she, too, seemed to relax. But, when I looked down at her, there were tears running down her chubby cheeks. I put an arm around her to pull her close to me when she looked up at me and said in the sincerity only of a child, "Mommie, I want to send Colonel Glenn a gold star, because he is such a great guy!"

I hope, Sir, you won't feel that we are being at all facetious. To a four year old a gold star is the epitome of praise for a job well done. So, please accept it, sent humbly, but happily!

Accept also, the thanks of parents with children who will grow up in a world that is bound to be better for having men like you, Sir, and your fellow Astronauts on our side.

From a Woman in Long Island, New York

Last night as I listened to the 11:15 news broadcast and heard your statement to the Senate about your religious faith, I felt compelled to write and tell you how much it really meant to me. You said more in those few sentences than many ministers can say in an hour and I was indeed thrilled as I listened to you. If our young people need a good example, they will never find a better one than you are.

Your deep humility should be a lesson to all of us. I have heard the quotation, "Great men never feel great, small men never feel small". You are indeed a great man.

I feel you have accomplished more toward leading men into unashamedly believing in Almighty God than hundreds of preachers can do; indeed, your life is your sermon.

Thank you from the bottom of my heart for giving us a message I will never forget.

This is just one of millions all over the world who wish you and your wonderful family the very best; you people are indeed an inspiration to all.

From a Woman in Milwaukee, Wisconsin

Last summer when I was vacationing at Streza on Lake Maggiore in Italy, I was sitting in the little Park across from my hotel reading when a group of twelve or thirteen young Italian boys and girls came along. They were on a hiking tour, and since they had a guitar, they stopped and "serenaded" this little white haired lady. Ever since that, one of the group—a young Italian girl of only fifteen years of age—has been writing me in Italian. I have to have her letters translated for me here at the bank building where I have an accounting office. The letters are beautifully expressed, and since you were the main subject in the letter just received this last week and since she has expressed so very well the feeling of her friends, I am taking the liberty of quoting from her letter:

"I have really been terribly thrilled by the great adventure of your astronaut, John Glenn. I have followed all the steps of the blast-off, first on the radio and then in the evening on television. I like him so much, not only for his unbelievable exploit, but also for himself personally, because among all the big crowd he looked more like a shy young man than a National hero, and when they cheered him, he would smilingly step aside to show off first one and then the other of his family. I believe he is an exceptional man, and he was so self-effacing, and he looked as if he didn't think he was worthy of the great and sudden triumph."

Because this comes from a young Italian girl, I have felt that I really should send it on to you. It so beautifully expresses the great admiration that not only your compatriots but your millions of "friends" all over the world feel about you and your great accomplishment.

From a Woman in Canton, Ohio

I would like to congratulate you and say we in Ohio are very proud of you. Thanks also for being so grand about the parades and all. Must be rather relaxing to get back to normal.

May I say that I think you folks and the other astronauts and their families will be at least partially responsible for a great new move-

237

ment. The rebirth of religion and patriotism. In a time when people seem to be ashamed to publicly express their belief in God, it was wonderful to hear you speak of your faith. The flight of Freedom 7, Liberty Bell 7, and Friendship 7 have done much to remind us of the nearness of God. I believe that most of the world was united in a single prayer at each blastoff and possibly through each flight.

Your expression of feeling for our country is very important too. You will be the people many youngsters and teenagers will be watching and listening to. You also helped give many parents a boost in morale and the reassurance of their own thoughts.

Col. Glenn, you're a man's man, a child's hero, and a mother's vision of her own son. For a space man, you're a very down to earth person.

From a Widow in Washington, D. C.

Of course you will receive thousands of letters on this wonderful day, but I feel that I, too, must send you a proud line to tell you how proud I again am of being a Marine. My father was a Colonel of Marines and my husband was a General, and gave his life, finally, to save others.

Thank you for adding still another act to make us prouder of our Corps!

From a First-Grade Teacher in Reno, Nevada

Your flight could not have been better timed for my first grade.

We had just finished a space unit and the children had made an evening trip to the observatory on the campus of the University of Nevada.

The children have been so interested in your flight. They have cut out all the pictures from the newspapers and brought them to school. We put them on the reading charts which the children dictated to me.

One mother at P.T.A. said "My daughter no longer comes running to kiss mother hello at breakfast. Instead she asks "Has Glenn gone up this morning yet" as she dashes for the morning paper".

You really put my children in orbit. The charts which were mailed to you from the First Grade at ___, Reno, Nevada were all their very first efforts at self expression in writing. I gave them chart paper, flow pens and let them go on their own. Their first stories and pictures were so natural that I wanted you and Mrs. Glenn to have them. Of course we had to wait for the P.T.A. meeting so all the parents could see them first.

You cannot imagine how much learning and real pride in our countrys' accomplishment has come to our first grade by your successful flight. Your many delays only helped the children learn the word 'maybe'.

From a Young Man in Macon, Georgia

Having been in a high school band, I loved playing the "Marine's Hymn" and was wondering how a fighting, cussing marine would ever "guard the streets of Heaven".

After becoming acquainted with you (on T.V.), I think that it might be possible.

America is a better place to live because of you Sir! Congratulations! And May God's blessings be yours now and always.

From a Woman in New England

As a group of American women concerned with the forces that are threatening the very survival of our nation we have been deeply grateful for the achievement which you symbolize in the conquest of space for our nation. Over and above this conquest, however, we are, as all American citizens must be, thrilled by your simple and moving words of devotion to our Flag uttered before the American

Congress. Your tribute to our Flag comes as welcome music to a generation beset by efforts to lower the Stars and Stripes in favor of a godless internationalism. Not since the day when another great American officer appeared before the American Congress to express a similar dedication to our great nation have the American people been afforded such an inspiring message.

Young Parents from LaCrosse, Washington, Write:

My husband and I are in our early twenties and we are the parents of two very small children. We live on a small farm in Washington State. We simply could not resist writing to you to offer our small, but heartfelt, congratulations.

The national and international news seems to become blacker and bleaker each day. The news of the horrible bombs, iron and bamboo curtains, cold and hot wars, communist threat, subversion and corruption makes us wonder what kind of a future our little girls might have.

Then came the wonderful news of your successful and historic flight into space. We can't tell you how proud we are of you, not only as a very brave soldier, but as a loyal and gracious man. Please forgive the American public for being a little silly and sentimental, but we needed a hero badly. And you, Col. Glenn, filled the bill far and above our wildest dreams. Indeed, you reminded us how very lucky we are to live in this great country, under God!

From a Teacher in Columbus, Ohio

While the eyes, hearts, and souls of America were upon you pouring out well deserved praise, no utterance could have been more sincere than that of a nine year old student boy of mine who said, "Miss Brown, I just *hated* my red hair until I found out that Col. Glenn has it, too. Now I'm *proud* I have it." You see, you've reached so many.

Thank you for making it possible for me to share a touch of greatness with my children through your most generous reply. Your greatness lies, not so much in what you have accomplished but rather, in the sincere, God-fearing person that you are. And this was not a TEAM effort! This influence has a greater effect than the most powerful nuclear warhead or a two-hundred orbital flight for it makes sense to the formative minds of youth.

THANK YOU!

From a Young Woman in Foxboro, Massachusetts

My father also served in the armed services. He was killed-in-action in Germany in 1945, when I was a few months old. Many is the time that I feel that he and all the other dead died in vain. It is when I see the United States as a free and democratic nation, thanks to the efforts of all servicemen, push forward as it did on February 20, that I know the truth. Your flight has become a symbol to me of the triumphs of our country and helps, at least in part, to justify the fate of my father and so many like him.

I am speechless with pride and admiration and I know that my father would be too, were he here. God bless you and best of luck in the future.

From a Woman in Grand Island, Nebraska

To Mr. & Mrs. Glenn, Sr.

Now that you've had a day to catch your breath, could a friendly stranger add her small word to the acclaim? We are all so proud of your son, and so happy that he has been honored for his courage,

241

but more than that, we are thankful to you, his parents, for making him what he is. America has needed a grass-roots hero for so long, and your John is filling the bill so perfectly that I feel I owe you a note of thanks.

It is an odd thing that mankind sometimes gets mired down in troubles of his own contrivance, and can find no way out; then, just before the water closes over his head, a straw comes along to give him hope and the boost that he needs to lift himself out. Probably nobody in planning the space program had any intention of making old-fashioned patriotism fashionable again in this dark void where so many are trying to tell us that being a staunch American is just a little bit nasty, but as it turns out, God has been very good to us, and has made a minor miracle in that the man who left this earth and came back is so thoroughly steeped in love of God and Country that it seems to be catching on with the people who worship him. I can truly believe that in that sense, John, Jr., is a messenger straight from God Himself. How proud you must be to have had the opportunity to help him become what he is.

From a Woman in Middletown, Rhode Island

Now that the noise and confusion of the parades is past I wonder if you might, perhaps, wonder how the "quiet" people felt, who were not able to actively show their appreciation of your group's efforts in space. We here in this home sat together on the couch touching hands in order to share the tremendous emotional impact of the flights. I say the "flights" because the same procedure held true from the first of Cmdr. Shepard, through Virgil Grissom's and on to yours. We're ordinary people, from a small town, who have never seen a rocket (other than on Buck Rogers) yet we shared that precious moment of the future with you to the fullest. When the rocket lifted off of the earth and seemed to ease into the sky we all were silent, no cheers, just gratitude that it was a good beginning. We are not a very religious family, in the sense that we don't get out to church each week, but we truly prayed for you that day. I don't think it was in particularly formal language, but simply "please, God, let it succeed."

I'm thirty six, was married during the war and have seven children aged two to sixteen. I'm afraid I was feeling like forty six, until lately when I realized that my generation was actively "doing something" and was quite fit to do so. I've always been pleased to have had my family so young, for many selfish reasons, but now I have an even greater pride when I can point out to my teenagers (who must think me ancient) the patriotism, pride and ability of others between thirty and forty six. I feel like I'm part of the world again, and I want to thank you for that.

Mostly, the family would like to say that we have much greater confidence in the future now, that project Mercury has reaffirmed our faith in ourselves. Now, instead of sitting around waiting for the bomb to drop, we are going to start doing the things we've put off in our lethargy. We're making the move westward that we've always day dreamed about. We can do anything we set our minds to. We're young!

From a Young Woman in Maplewood, New Jersey

I have never felt as proud to be an American as I did today. I was so happy and proud to see that rocket go off successfully that the tears came streaming down my cheeks. I don't think you would know what Walter Cronkite said as you took off, so I will tell you. He just uttered three words which I believe truly expressed the feelings of every American at just that time: "Go, baby, go". He said it with such sincerity and earnestness.

I was so engrossed in the whole trip that I spent the hours of 8:00 A.M. to 4:00 P.M. glued to the television set. I didn't eat a thing but a bit of cereal until dinner-time. I taped most of the broadcast, and I am so proud to have it.

All the prayers of the American people were with you today, including mine. I sincerely hope that you enjoy as much happiness and luck in the future.

Most sincerely and gratefully,
A very proud citizen of the United States of America.

P.S. Tell your daughter, Lynn, that I truly hope she wins the election for president at her school.

243

From a Man in New York City

Once again I feel the pride of having worn the Marine uniform. I actually was not a member of the Corps, but a Seabee attached to the 1st Division during W. W. 2. If I had ever lost the pride of having served with the Corps, it was only mentally dormant. Your courage today awakened that pride once again.

If in the future I again hear the "Marines Hymn", you may rest assured that I shall stand "taller" than I have in the past wearing that uniform, and I feel that all Americans will follow suit. We Americans are a funny people, we forget too fast. I am sure that today we all remembered why you were up there. I only hope that we shall not forget it in the bleak future, not bleak for us, but for the enemy that is looking down the barrels of our weapons.

There are two things I learned during W. W. 2, one was the "CAN DO" spirit of the Seabees, and the other is the "Pride of the Marines", combining the both I know we have an unbeatable team.

From a Midshipman

To Colonel and Mrs. Glenn.

I would like to take a few minutes of your time to voice my sincere appreciation and admiration to you and your family in your handling of the events of the past few months.

Your exceptional example, sir, has provided all young officers with an impeccable criterion of conduct becoming of any man in the Military. By your outstanding devotion to your family, your country and your service, you have inspired so many of us to realize, more than ever, the importance and scope of our duty as defenders of this great country of ours. It is my sincerest wish, that some day, I may follow in the footsteps of you and your colleagues in making the United States, not only a world wide, but a universal power, and in preserving our precious doctrines of freedom and equality.

As for your part, Mrs. Glenn, you have greatly helped to alleviate the fear that so many of us have of asking a young woman to marry into the exacting position of a military wife. Your understanding *and devotion to your husband's duty, under the most extra-ordinary circumstances, has, indeed, been exemplary. I only hope that some day I may be blessed with a wife half as courageous as you have proven yourself to be.*

May I offer my sincerest thanks and best wishes for continued success in the years to come.

From a Retired Air Force Colonel in North Carolina

"The United States of America owes to Lt. Col. John Glenn U.S.M.C. a deep sense of gratitude and thanksgiving for accomplishing what *No President, No Politician* and *No Clergyman* has been able to do for America since Teddy Roosevelt.

By his unshackled patriotism and sincerity he has enabled us to reaffirm faith not only in ourselves, but in the United States of America and in Almighty God."

Sir, I salute you—

From a Woman in Altoona, Pennsylvania

My husband and I wish to send our congratulations to you and thank you for what you have done for our country—your successfully courageous feat was the shot "in the arm" that our country needed.

Personally, my husband who has been shut in by illness for seven months got a tremendous lift out of your whole big day; he was "glued" to the TV thru the entire proceedings and "signed off" at 11:15 that night with the last news coverage.

Me, I should have known better after seeing you going to and from church on various Sundays before, but when your voice was coming over so clearly and steady from the capsule, I thought, "Here is a pretty cold fish, probably practically mechanical without much human emotion"; but when at Cocoa Beach you greeted your wife as "Annie" and cried a little, then and there my opinion changed and I thought, "What a real guy". Then, later at the Cape when you were showing your family the inside of the capsule, you were so kind and gentle with all, especially your mother, well, Colonel, we shed a few tears, too.

In this very modern age, when real family life has seemed to be just something to joke about, and ma and pa are just old folks, you

246

really put status again in family relations. Also, where children, especially teen-agers are stamped as brazen and show-offy, it was nice to see your nice quiet boy and lovely feminine daughter showed affection by you, but never ahead of your wife or parents.

May all good things happen to you and you live, as you said, "every day as your last on earth", and we know you'll still be one of the best things our old world has known.

From a Woman Pre-Medical Student

I am writing this letter as one of many grateful Americans, all of whom are rejoicing over your recent orbital flight.

However, there is another, more important, reason for my writing to you. I didn't write to Cmdr. Shepard or to Capt. Grissom, and it is for that very reason that I am writing to you. Here is the story. Although I was not privileged to see Capt. Grissom take off, I was up many mornings to see both you and Cmdr. Shepard leave the launch pad. Although my excitement grew steadily and more uncontrollable when I realized that you were actually staying up there in orbit, I must in all truthfulness confess that I have never, in all my life, been as thrilled as I was on that first sub-orbital flight of Cmdr. Shepard's. It was something that no American had ever seen before, nor had ever dreamed of seeing, and I honestly believe that as long as I live, tears will come to my eyes when I remember that 15-minute journey, and see that launching in my mind's eye.

Please do not misinterpret my feelings, Colonel Glenn, for here is what I mean. You are not a physically supreme person for the feat which you accomplished for the free world, but you ARE a supremely ethical and unselfish person, and that is why this letter is being written. To be brief, I am saying Thank You for not taking that first memory away from me. Thank you for not minimizing it in the eyes of one who thought it was the greatest accomplishment which man had yet achieved. Thank you for including Cmdr. Shepard and Capt. Grissom in your success, and Thank You for paving the way for future astronauts to receive as much cooperation and as many prayers as you did. For THIS, you are truly a hero.

247

From an Eighty-Eight-Year-Old British Man

Like the rest of the world I was thrilled with your triple journey round the earth and offer you my sincere congratulations on so epic a deed. I am glad to read that you suffered no after-effects from the speed and altitude.

You can in all truth say of yourself, like Hamlet, "I could be bounded in a nutshell, and count myself a King of infinite space."

16, SPRING STREET,
STOCKTON ON-TEES,
Co. DURHAM.
24. 2. 62.

Dear Sir,

Like the rest of the
world I was thrilled with
your triple journey round the
earth and offer you my
sincere congratulations on so
epic a deed. I am glad to
read that you suffered no
after-effects from the speed
and altitude.

You can in all truth
say of yourself, like Hamlet,

" I could be bounded in a
nutshell, and count myself
a King of infinite space."

(Act II, Scene II)

I wish you the best of
luck in any further journeys
into space.

Yours sincerely,
John Cowley.
aged 88 years

Lt Col. John Glenn,
Cape Canaveral;
Florida,
U.S.A.